LARRY JACOBSON, EdD, JD

INSTA-TRUST

THE PROVEN
TRUST-BUILDING
PROCESS TO
CREATE INSTANT
RAPPORT &
LONG-TERM
RELATIONSHIPS

Published and Distributed by
SOUND WISDOM
PO Box 310
Shippensburg, PA 17257-0310
717-530-2122
info@soundwisdom.com
www.soundwisdom.com

ISBN 13 TP: 978-1-64095-433-5
ISBN 13 eBook: 978-1-64095-434-2

For Worldwide Distribution, Printed in the U.S.A.

1 2 3 4 5 6 / 28 27 26 25 24 23 22

"THE KEY TO MOST SUCCESSFUL RELATIONSHIPS IS THE ABILITY TO CREATE FAST TRUST WITH INDIVIDUALS YOU HAVE NEVER MET."

Dr. Larry Jacobson

"IN TODAY'S SNAPSHOT WORLD, THOSE WHO SUCCEED ARE THOSE WHO MASTER THE ART OF INSTA-TRUST."

Dr. Larry Jacobson

For my wife Cindy, who puts up with my eccentricities and is the best thing that ever happened to me.

THE FOUNDATION OF BUILDING TRUST IS YOUR RESPONSIBILITY

"True genius resides in the capacity for evaluation of uncertain, hazardous, and conflicting information."

This was said by the late, great Winston Churchill. Let me add: True trust exists only when doubt has been eliminated.

It took me well over a decade from the beginning of my professional career to learn that solely logical and methodical approaches in interacting with my clients were not the best way to build trust and relationships. My professional training was at the MBA program at the University of Chicago and at the Georgetown University Law Center. My education was decades prior to the explosion of the development of behavioral economics/social psychology concepts that conclusively debunked the notion that our decision making is based only on self-interest and logic. Concepts such as risk aversion, recency bias, confirmation bias and the overconfidence effect were not part of my lexicon.

A few years after I became a partner in my law firm, I finally figured out that the purportedly logical corporate executives, professionals at professional service firms and entrepreneurs I represented were far from emotionless in their decision making. By decision making, I mean the critical decisions they make in their business and their critical decision to hire their professionals. Meaning ME. I figured this out once and for all when I participated in a typical "beauty contest" where a company was looking to hire outside tax counsel. My presentation was professionally flawless. And my presentation was as colorless as a backyard snowman. Notwithstanding that I really was the most qualified individual to serve this company on the matter with which they needed assistance, I did not get the assignment. I was fortunate enough to receive feedback from the person at the meeting who recommended my participation in the "beauty contest." He told me that while his fellow executives were looking for someone with technical expertise (which they could see I had), they were also concerned that I was not reaching them on a human level. More precisely, they wanted to work with someone who gave the impression that they were ready to "go to war" with them. That feedback was the turning point where I made sure that all future interactions had not only a technical component, but also a substantial emotional connection.

A few years later, I was involved in a very contentious and highly technical Tax Court case. The amount of money in dispute was over $70,000,000, and every month interest was compounding in the hundreds of thousands of dollars on the potential liability. Even though my client was a public company, the amount in dispute was sizable.

The attorney representing the Internal Revenue Service was a stereotypical representative of the IRS. She was looking at reeling in a huge win to bolster her government career for life. She had no desire to settle the case for any amount, let alone an amount that would recognize the hazards of litigation. On the other hand, I felt highly confident that we had a strong case. Even so, I recognized that any court case is never a slam dunk winner and that if we had the ability to settle it for a reasonable amount, our client should seriously consider it.

Around a year before the trial date, I was asked to meet with the client's Board of Directors to discuss the status of the case, the likelihood of success and the possible settlement approaches. I knew only two of the Board members, the Chairman and the Chief Financial Officer, and I had met the Chairman only a few times before the meeting. Basically, I was meeting with those two and ten additional strangers. None of the Board members had any knowledge of tax law and two of the Board members had a nonprofit background and therefore little knowledge of corporate finance. So I was going into a meeting of tremendous importance to the corporation with little personal connection with the participants.

When I was asked to present, I introduced myself and gave around a 15-second statement of my qualifications. Then I told the group that the tax matter was highly complex and offered to explain the matter to them in nontechnical terms. A couple of Board members asked me to do so, and I spent the next five minutes breaking down a technical tax dispute in language that a high school junior could understand (my strong belief is if a professional cannot explain a matter to a client or patient in language that a high school junior can understand, they ought to retire). Once I finished that presentation, I explained the personality of the IRS attorney I would be going up against. I portrayed her as a schoolyard bully who used intimidation as a method to win her cases. I equated her to Javert, the policeman in *Les Misérables* who was fanatical about trying to track down Valjean, who stole a loaf of bread to feed his starving family over a course of a couple of decades. I told the Board that we were the Valjean in our story; we were in the ethical and legal right, and we were not going let a bully get in our way. That story got the Board's attention very quickly.

I then moved the Board to focus on probabilities of successfully winning the case. But initially, I did not do so in dry mathematical lingo. I noted we had unlimited resources, so the IRS could not outspend us and the IRS (due to self-imposed budgetary constraints) could not obtain expert witnesses of the caliber I lined up. To give them a visual representation, I poured two glasses of water with equal amounts of water in each glass. I then poured about two-thirds of the water from one glass into the other. I pointed out that the glass with the lower amount of water was around one-sixth of the total water of both glasses. I stated with authority that the glass with the lower amount of water represented the likelihood the IRS would win the case. On the basis of that physical presentation, I recommended to the Board that they make a one-time offer to settle the case for one-sixth of the amount of dispute and, if the IRS did not settle, to take the case to trial. After a few questions, the Board accepted my recommendation.

At the time, I was a junior partner, and if I was wrong and we lost the case, it easily could have cost me my position at my law firm. So my trust building had a technical component, an emotional component and a quiet confidence component. I needed to demonstrate quiet confidence in order to win over the Board, as it was an unstated assumption among everyone in the room that if we failed, my law firm (and likely I) could possibly be terminated as outside counsel. But unlike the IRS attorney, my position was not based on emotion, even if part of my presentation was emotionally based. The Board sensed my confidence and, after my presentation, was willing to bet on me.

The Board's faith in me was justified. We tried the case, and before the judge adjourned the trial, he asked the IRS counsel and our team if we wanted to meet him in chambers to hear his honest assessment of the case. I didn't even hesitate and agreed to meet with him. The IRS attorney refused to meet with us and the judge in chambers. That is when I knew we had slayed the bully. The judge ultimately held completely in our favor, and our client owed zero taxes. Obviously our client was ecstatic, and I received a huge career boost. But it all was due to my ability to convince a nervous Board to have faith in me and my abilities.

What I learned from this critical career turning-point moment is that making an emotional connection is vital even in front of the most seasoned businessmen and businesswomen. If I had not incorporated emotional-level trust building in my presentation to the Board, my career might have taken an entirely different path. You may face a similar situation in your professional career. Think about how many more great opportunities you might gain if you are able to balance the emotional and logical aspects of gaining the trust of those who don't previously know you. Are you ready?

You and I live in a world where people, be they professionals, clients, customers or the general public, make snap judgments about those they come into contact with. You can complain all you want about the "social media" society or short attention spans or you can adjust to the world as it exists. The key to most successful professional relationships is the ability to create fast trust with individuals you have never met.

That's what this book is all about.

Many of our initial interactions with clients or customers are not face-to-face. They might be by phone, email or video chat. Recent technological and demographic shifts have accelerated the magnitude and importance of developing a skill set as to how to build fast trust with others in important business settings. What has not changed—and what will never change—is the critical importance of building fast rapport, connection and trust in professional settings. **This is true whether you are meeting in person or virtually.** If a client or important business contact does not trust you, either the relationship does not commence or it gets off to such a rocky start that repairing the relationship will take valuable time and is not certain to occur.

Sticking to the virtual setting for a moment, as a medical professional or dental specialist meeting with a potential patient via video chat, how do you establish trust so that the potential patient feels that they can trust you with their care? As an attorney negotiating a big corporate deal or litigation settlement and speaking to your counterparty for the first time by phone, how do you establish quick trust so that the other side feels they can ultimately reach a fair agreement? If you are an architect or engineer, how do you build trust in an initial virtual meeting where the potential client truly has no knowledge of the technical issues involved in how you perform your job?

The bottom line is that in today's world, the ability of a professional to build "Insta-Trust" (as the term is defined later in this book) is as important a skill as the technical requirements of your profession. You can be the most skilled oral surgeon, attorney or CPA, but if you cannot relate to potential patients, clients and other professionals, you will be bereft of individuals to serve or represent.

Getting back to Churchill's comment, one of the greatest flaws that each of us has is that we think that we can size up another person very quickly. You think that you can analyze their personality, their mindset, their objectives and their needs in a matter of seconds or minutes. In fact, nothing is further from the truth. You really know nothing (or very little) about a stranger prior to a first meeting. Sure you might do a little due diligence or a referral source might tell you a little about the person you are about to speak with. The reality is you truly don't know the person you are about to get on a video chat with or meet in person (or if you know them slightly, you don't know their mindset with respect to this particular matter). As importantly, they know little or nothing about you.

Thus, your first task in any initial meeting is to build trust. Not to show off genius, not to hard sell, not to come off as robotic and definitely not to come off as though your time is so valuable that the person you are speaking with is a commodity. You need to gain their confidence before you gain their trust. YOU MUST DEVELOP AN INSTA-TRUST MINDSET. This book explains exactly how to develop an Insta-Trust mindset.

The purpose of this book is to share my trust secrets on how to build immediate trust in professional settings. This could be with potential patients or clients. It could be with government officials you interact with on behalf of clients. It could be with individuals you negotiate with on behalf of clients. It could be with referral sources. This book is geared toward helping you with the wide variety of virtual situations you encounter in which you might have five minutes to make a strong first impression. In many situations, trust assessment might occur in as little as 120 seconds. In today's snapshot world, those who succeed are those who master the art of Insta-Trust. And as shown later, those who successfully build Insta-Trust are those who have a teaching and curiosity mindset. Those closed-minded individuals who open conversations trying to impress others with their credentials are doomed to failure.

This book is specially addressed to the needs of licensed professionals such as physicians, dental specialists, attorneys, CPAs, engineers and architects. But the concepts in this book can also apply to all salespersons and deal makers (such as brokers, realtors and investment bankers). If you work in a field where building quick trust is essential to your professional success, this book is for you. For the purposes of this book, you are a professional if you are an expert in your field and a client or patient is coming to you either (1) for advice, (2) to have you perform a procedure or service, (3) for a physical deliverable (such as a tax return or building plan) or (4) to negotiate on their behalf.

You might ask why I am qualified to be your guide for the next 150 or so pages. I have been engaging in these techniques for over 30 years, first as a partner in a large Chicago-based law firm and for the last seven years as a consultant who negotiates the sale of dental specialty practices. Both as an attorney and as a consultant, I have over 50,000 hours of representing clients and negotiating deals with people around the world whom I never met in person. In the early 1990s, I mastered the techniques of how to build virtual trust in a wide array of situations and with a wide variety of personality types.

I took this knowledge and commenced doctoral studies with a desire to engage in research in virtual trust building. In 2014, I defended my doctoral thesis, titled "You Take Them As You Find Them: An Examination Of How Negotiators Build Trust With Parties They Never Meet Face-To-Face." So the concepts in this book are a blend of practical knowledge based on over 40 years of personal experience and research-based findings in my doctoral thesis.

However impressive my experience might be, I would not be walking the walk in terms of the core concept of building trust if my aim was to lecture you. I am your guide, not your lecturer. You and I will take this journey together, as ultimately my goal is for you to be successful in building quick trust with those whose interests are important. For your success will be my success. Let's get started.

I UNDERSTAND TRUST AS A PROFESSIONAL AND AS A PERSON. AS A FATHER AND AS A LAWYER. I LIVE IT EVERY DAY.

THIS BOOK IS ABOUT LEARNING, APPLYING, EARNING AND KEEPING ONE OF THE MOST IMPERATIVE ELEMENTS OF LIFE.

TABLE OF CONTENTS

|NTRODUCTION|

NO ONE REALLY KNOWS

"Out of intense complexities intense simplicities emerge."
- Winston Churchill

An oral surgeon receives a referral from one of her referring dentists asking her to remove an impacted wisdom tooth. The referral sheet is transmitted to the oral surgeon via email and has information regarding the problem. The tooth is infected, and the oral surgeon is likely to have to use mild to substantial anesthesia to make the patient comfortable when removing the tooth. The referral slip has no information regarding how the patient tolerates dental pain or anything else about the patient's personality. The oral surgeon is getting ready for a short video chat with the patient to discuss the procedure.

How should the oral surgeon proceed? The obvious objective of the video chat is to explain the procedure to the patient and the various options available in terms of pain management during the procedure. That is the technical end of the discussion. However, where most professionals fall far short is recognizing that most patients/clients are more interested at the outset in learning about them as a person than in learning the nuts and bolts of how the professional does their work. Do you really think most of your patients or clients care about how you prepare briefs or documents, draw building plans, develop tax strategies or pull teeth? In the vast majority of situations, the *how* of a professional's technique is irrelevant to the person sitting in front of you. The potential client or patient already assumes you know what you are doing. They are far more concerned with who you are as a person than whether you can use your knowledge to solve their problem.

Patients, clients and negotiating counterparties make quick first impressions. Those first impressions involve sizing up the other person as to whether they are trustworthy. Only once trust is established can a professional relationship commence.

In this example, we have a highly competent oral surgeon about to speak to a new (and likely nervous) patient about a pretty significant, invasive procedure. The oral surgeon knows nothing about the patient (other than the dental problem), and the patient likely knows little or nothing about the procedure. The process moving forward is quite simple. The oral surgeon (and any professional commencing a potential business relationship) should start from the mindset that NO ONE REALLY KNOWS.

"ANY PROFESSIONAL COMMENCING A POTENTIAL BUSINESS RELATIONSHIP SHOULD START FROM THE MINDSET THAT NO ONE REALLY KNOWS."

– Dr. Larry Jacobson

What do I mean by NO ONE REALLY KNOWS? In the case of the oral surgeon, she should start by assuming she knows zero about the personality, mindset or objectives of the patient. Personality can only be gleaned upon significant interaction with the patient. Mindset relates to whether the patient is willing to proceed with the matter at hand if convinced it is in their best interest. Objectives are what the patient hopes to achieve by having the oral surgeon do her job with excellence and a minimum level of discomfort.

In this case, the oral surgeon knows nothing about the personality or mindset of the prospective patient. How does she build trust quickly? The oral surgeon should understand the difference between empathy and connection and know which is most important in the initial stages of a relationship. The need to build connection applies to all professional settings. Empathy is showing feeling for the other person and their situation. Connection is the creation of an emotional bond between the professional and their patient/client. Showing empathy can take place after you develop an emotional connection.

Once the video chat starts, the oral surgeon should take 30 to 45 seconds to introduce herself and acknowledge that she read the referral slip sent by the patient's dentist. This is the same if you are a business professional and have received a referral. Firstly, the oral surgeon should give the introduction in a quietly confident manner. Even though the patient and oral surgeon know nothing about each other, research and practice show a strong correlation between trusting relationships and a confident personality. So the oral surgeon should convey quiet confidence at the outset. Quiet confidence is having a steady personality where the professional shows he or she knows their stuff without being overbearing. Boisterous confidence is counterproductive and destructive. Quiet confidence shows that the professional is not only highly competent but also that they are patient- or client-centered. On the other hand, boisterous confidence shows the professional is ego-driven and not patient- or client-centered. Which one do you exhibit most?

Once the oral surgeon introduces herself and acknowledges the problem at hand, the next step, since she knows nothing about the patient, is to ask a series of open-ended patient-oriented questions. "How long has this been bothering you? Did your dentist explain how I can be of assistance? What is your pain tolerance level?

Have you been under anesthesia previously? How did you respond to anesthesia? Does going under sedation cause you angst?"

These questions obviously have a professional component; the oral surgeon has a need to understand the patient's view of anesthesia, as sedation is a procedure with potentially very serious complications, including, very rarely, death. Yet the most important element of patient- or client-centered questioning is to demonstrate a deep concern about the patient or client. Whether you are a health care provider or a professional such as an attorney, accountant, engineer, architect, consultant or deal maker, your questions need to demonstrate that you are creating solutions for THEM. As these questions are asked, the patient or client needs to see and hear firsthand the confidence and competency level of the oral surgeon. The patient needs to see and hear that the oral surgeon is concerned about the patient as a human being and not as a profit center. The patient can begin to develop trust in the oral surgeon; the same is true in any non-health-care setting.

The following is a list of questions that can be asked (with the appropriate tweaks depending on your specific profession) to build a personal connection with the person with whom you are trying to build trust:

1. What do you think the problem is that brings us together today?

2. On a scale of 1 to 10, what is the pain or concern level that this problem is causing you?

3. When we are successful in solving your problem, please provide a colorful description of how our solution will positively impact your life (or organization)?

4. How quickly do we need to get your problem solved?

5. Are there impediments or other factors that might prevent us from getting the problem solved in the most effective manner?

6. Can you please tell me three bad experiences with prior professionals that turned you off? Can you please tell me three good experiences with prior professionals that made you likely to be enthusiastic to work with them?

Getting back to the example, once the oral surgeon asks her questions and receives the associated answers, she still must work harder to build quick trust. The answers are helpful, but the oral surgeon still has a lot of work to do in figuring out the patient's personality type and how to build quick trust with this patient. The next step is for the oral surgeon to describe the procedure in terms tailored for this patient, including how she makes the patient most comfortable (and in this case the incredible care she takes in safely administering anesthesia). The information is conveyed in simple layman's terms and in a matter-of-fact, confident manner.

What happens next is the key to building quick trust. At this point, the oral surgeon asks the patient if they understood what she said and then asks the patient about their concerns about what will happen when they come in for their procedure. A professional should never hesitate to ask in multiple ways at different times during the conversation whether the patient or client understands what is being discussed and whether they have additional questions. By asking and getting questions answered, the oral surgeon achieves three objectives. First, she gets a strong sense of the patient's real and imagined concerns about the procedure. Second, she gets a better sense of the personality type of the patient so as to better interact with the patient before, during and after the procedure. Third, this approach builds trust. It shows the patient that the oral surgeon is patient-centered and cares about them as a human being. **You can use this exact process to show your clients you care and to start building trust.**

This process all starts from the premise that the professional goes into an initial conversation with a prospective client or patient with zero preconceived notions regarding that individual. When I was doing my research for my dissertation, a sage attorney told me that he starts out new relationships with a blank canvas. By that he meant that he assumed nothing about the other person and started from a default position that the other person wants to explore a professional relationship. He said that his antenna is always up for integrity issues, but he assumes the other person is acting in good faith until proven otherwise.

So what does trust really mean in an initial meeting? Most people equate trust with integrity. Yes, integrity is an important element of trust. However, there is no way any human being can make a totally accurate assessment of another person's truthfulness quickly. Assessing the other person's real truthfulness quickly (except in rare situations where you have 100 percent factual evidence that the other person is bullshitting you, and in that case you stop the conversation and move on) just doesn't happen. Thus, integrity assessment is a function of how trust is developed at other levels.

Initial trust building focuses on things that the other person can assess quickly, whether in person, by phone, by email or by video chat. As developed in depth later in the book, there are three elements of trust that can be assessed quickly by another person. First is whether you appear to be competent. Second is using active listening to glean the concerns (real, imagined, material and psychological) of the other person. Third is demonstrating a collaborative mindset where your role is not as a savior, a savant or a soothsayer, but as a partner working with the other person to help solve their problem. Quick trust can be built even before integrity assessments as long the competency, active listening and collaborative approaches are used by the professional.

The final important concept in this chapter involves a teaching mindset in terms of quick trust building. When you start to build trust, think of yourself as a teacher. You have knowledge the other side doesn't have, but you don't know their knowledge base or learning style. Great teachers do not come off as "know-it-alls"; they teach in a manner that is designed to maximize the ability of the student to understand the subject matter and feel comfortable asking questions if they get stuck. As a teacher and professional, my job is to figure out your personality and what you need to learn so I can teach you about the ways you and I can work together to SOLVE YOUR PROBLEM. This is true whether you are a medical or dental professional, an attorney, a CPA, an engineer or a negotiator. If you take an educator mindset into your trust-building encounters, you have a high success rate in terms of client retention and satisfaction.

"THERE IS NO WAY ANY HUMAN BEING CAN MAKE A TOTALLY ACCURATE ASSESSMENT OF ANOTHER PERSON'S TRUTHFULNESS QUICKLY."

Dr. Larry Jacobson

IMPORTANT NOTE: This book specifically addresses the needs of licensed professionals. Examples are used for physicians, dental specialists, attorneys, CPAs, engineers and architects. But EVERY matter discussed here can be applied to salespeople and deal makers (brokers, insurance agents, realtors and investment bankers). No matter who you are or what you are trying to achieve in business and life, it requires trust and trustworthiness.

Chapter One describes how trust should be the primary outcome of your first interaction and how everything good comes from that mindset. Chapter One also describes the Wheels of Insta-Trust™. The Bridge discusses the role of emotion in building relationships. Chapter Two discusses the 11 personality archetypes you will be interacting with when building Insta-Trust. Chapter Three discusses how trust is earned and not "sold" in the early stages of a business relationship. It also discusses the need to do your homework on the prospective patient/client to the extent possible before the first interaction. Chapter Four is pure trust insight—how and why your bullshit meter is always running (and so is theirs). Chapter Five lays out the attributes of an excellent trusting relationship. Chapter Six takes you to the first step of trust building in showing the prospect you care as much about them as you care about yourself.

Chapter Seven builds on Chapter Six by describing the second step of trust building in showing the importance of empathy. Chapter Eight details the third step of trust building by being an active listener, but not in a manipulative manner. Then comes an Interlude that builds on the iconic song by The Who ("Who Are You") and highlights how it is much easier to build trust when a great reputation precedes your first interaction with a patient or client. Chapter Nine is the critical fourth step of trust building. It's about listening until you can create a solution that works for the other person—and they trust you enough to move forward. Chapter Ten details the challenging fifth step of trust building, which is eliminating ego, the villain that prevents trusting relationships and win-win solutions. The Ending ties together the concepts in an integrated manner.

Since this book is written with a wide variety of professionals in mind, going forward, rather than referring to the potential person you are speaking with as a "patient," "client," "customer" or "negotiating counterparty," I will use the avatar of "Patricia" when I reference the person you are meeting for the first time and building Insta-Trust with. In this book, Patricia is the person whom you are trying to have hire you to work on a matter of importance to her or him or the person you are negotiating with to achieve a successful solution.

I have put together a workbook that allows you to implement the important concepts in this book. To obtain your free copy, please go to www.insta-trust.com.

To ensure complete understanding, many chapters end with questions to ask yourself regarding the concepts discussed in that chapter. I find in my teaching and training that students are more likely to apply well-thought-out questions than pithy admonitions. Each question is addressed to you personally and is designed to make you think about how you can better improve some level of trust building.

Ask Yourself

QUESTION ONE: Do I approach each new interaction with openness and no preconceptions?

QUESTION TWO: Am I willing to spend at least two-thirds of an initial interaction listening rather than talking?

QUESTION THREE: Am I coming off as treating the other person as an individual and not as a checklist?

QUESTION FOUR: Am I constantly monitoring how I am coming across to the other side in my initial interaction?

QUESTION FIVE: Am I displaying quiet confidence throughout my interactions?

QUESTION SIX: Am I putting the other person first through my tone and language?

QUESTION SEVEN: Am I displaying an educational mindset in my discussions with the other person?

TELL YOURSELF...I understand the concepts described in each chapter and I believe I can use these concepts to build lasting trust from the opening moments of any meeting or conversation.

|O1|

TRUST IS YOUR OUTCOME; IT LEADS TO YOUR INCOME

"You are not Vincent van Gogh."
– Dr. Larry Jacobson

Don't you hate to be sold? Doesn't it make you feel cheap and unwanted? You bet. What does it mean to be sold? It's simply when the salesperson conveys little interest in you, your problem and your solution, and gives the impression they are a whole lot more concerned about how much money they are going to make off of selling you a good or service. They convey an attitude that what is good for them must be good for you. Of course, nothing is further from the truth. Your bullshit meter is on super high when you are being played.

Trust never occurs when a potential customer or client feels they're being sold. Trust in new relationship situations does not begin with a sales pitch. Trust begins with an educational process on both sides' part. Trust builds slowly and can be lost quickly. Trust gathers steam when the client begins to let their guard down and talks freely about their real concerns. When trusting relationships build, it is like a snowball rolling downhill with speed. In other words, great momentum leads to a powerful result.

Trust is your desired outcome. It is your only initial outcome. If you can succeed in building trust with a potential client or a negotiating counterparty, the odds are heavy in your favor that you will achieve a result that meets their needs and then your financial and business needs. Rarely will your business result arise where trust is not built first. Sure there are situations where a potential client or counterparty is so desperate that they are willing to do anything you ask them to do. But those situations are few and far between. More importantly, ask yourself if you are so interested in a sale that you are willing to take advantage of another party. Because you might win a small battle but lose the long war. Why?

TRUST IS YOUR DESIRED OUTCOME. IT IS YOUR ONLY INITIAL OUTCOME.

In the professional sphere, reputation is everything. Social media and online reviews allow aggrieved persons to vent about how poorly they are treated. Yes, not all reviews or posts are accurate, and some might be outright defamatory. However, if there is a pattern of negative comments about you and how you treat patients or clients, it becomes far more challenging for you to build the reputation of being a trustworthy professional. You start an initial virtual interaction with the equivalent of a ten-pound weight on your leg. It takes a lot of work to overcome that type of obstacle in building initial trust. Can it be done? Perhaps. But it takes a lot longer and the outcome of a trusting relationship is far from certain.

In terms of building a trust toolbox, ask yourself, what other professionals do you trust? Then ask yourself, why do you trust them? What processes did they use to build trust? How did they convey confidence and competence? What was their active listening style? Did they use humor or levity to show they sensed a key point where the discussion was getting tense? Did they use excellent segues to move from a relationship-building train of questions to a solution-building process? By observing other professionals and seeing how they build trust, you can decide which of their processes work best for you and begin to build your personal trust toolbox.

You can find quick trust-building techniques in the most peculiar areas. Reading biographies, especially those of military leaders and successful sports coaches, can help you find trust-focused nuggets of wisdom. In particular, military leaders' and coaches' interactions tend to be very short in nature; their ability to build trust is not based, contrary to popular belief, on power dynamics. Rather, outstanding military leaders and coaches know how to use 30- to 60-second interactions to build and rebuild trust with specific individuals. Think of memorable comments made to you and how they made you more trusting of that individual. Then think about how you can use similar stories or phrases that you mold to your unique situation. For example, there is a classic quote attributed to the legendary Green Bay Packers coach Vince Lombardi where he says, "I firmly believe that any man's finest hour, the greatest fulfillment of all that he holds dear, is the moment when he has worked his heart out in a good cause and lies exhausted on the field of battle, victorious." I use this quote frequently and tell the Patricias of the world that I will work to exhaustion, if necessary, to solve their problem.

You need to develop trust-building habits. Having a trust-building mindset enables you to naturally and seamlessly treat initial interactions with potential clients as an enjoyable and positive process. Many professionals are uncomfortable with having to meet with potential clients. They would rather just do the work. In this era, gifted professionals without client-servicing abilities are underemployed professionals. I tell my reticent clients that, "You are not Vincent van Gogh." By that I mean I am not judging their painting abilities. What I am judging is their extreme introversion. Van Gogh was an extreme introvert. His interactions, other than with a few other painters and a few family members, were nonexistent. He made no efforts to market himself and his works (unlike Picasso, who was an early adopter of the artist as a personal brand). Vincent had his brother Theo market his works. Yet during his lifetime, virtually none of his paintings were sold. Only after his death was van Gogh recognized for the genius he possessed.

"YOU CANNOT AFFORD TO IGNORE THE NEED TO HAVE A TRUST-BUILDING PERSONALITY UNLESS YOU PREFER TO BE LIKE VAN GOGH AND BEGIN MAKING SALES AFTER YOU ARE DEAD."

– Dr. Larry Jacobson

Professional excellence means nothing without clients. Today, outstanding professionals are those blessed with a combination of professional excellence and trust-building excellence. One without the other means the professional is not deeply committed to building a sustainable and meaningful professional practice.

In this era, building a trustworthy persona requires a professional to master the virtual tools that are being used in a larger percentage of initial client interactions. Although skill building in terms of how to use virtual techniques such as video conferencing, email and telephone are beyond the scope of this book, a few observations are appropriate. First, virtual interactions lack visual cues such as body language and clear facial expressions. Second, voice tone is not nearly as clear in virtual interactions as in in-person interactions. Third, when communicating by text or email, individuals tend to be brief and to the point. There tends to be little interpersonal interaction in written virtual communications.

Taking all of this into account, the trust-building professional needs to be very careful in terms of the language used in virtual interactions. Simple language is preferred and keeping questions and answers short is essential. Most importantly, be very, very careful about tone. Given the lack of nuance, professionals need to understand that their language must be so precise that it leaves little doubt that any reasonable client can understand what the professional is trying to convey and the tone of the conversation. When in doubt, keep in mind that in an initial conversation, the potential client is likely either nervous or truly uncertain about the professional's personality, collaborative approach and competence. Fancy language and a condescending attitude resonate even more negatively in a virtual setting. The mantra of truly not knowing the personality of the potential client and adjusting accordingly is even more necessary in virtual settings.

At this point, it is useful to discuss the WHEELS OF INSTA-TRUST™ that I developed for the purposes of this book. The circles are designed to demonstrate how various key concepts are intertwined in developing quick trust in many professional situations. The goal is to hit the sweet spot in the middle and become an Insta-Trust Impactor.

WHEELS OF INSTA-TRUST™

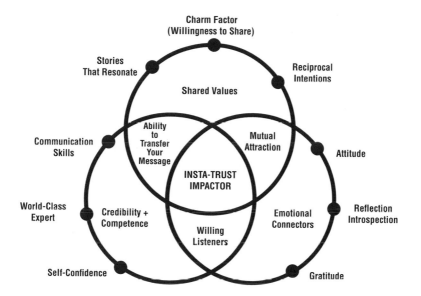

Each circle in the WHEELS OF INSTA-TRUST™ represents a key concept. The top circle represents Shared Values between a professional and a potential Patricia. They can be spoken or unspoken. The circle to the right represents Emotional Connectors between the professional and the potential patient/client. This is the process of making deep connections that go beyond linear or rational thought. The circle to the left represents the Credibility and Competence of the professional. It goes without saying that if the professional is not highly competent, no level of Shared Values or Emotional Connectors will lead to trust.

Shared Values can be conveyed in several different ways. The use of stories can get parties to ascertain and build Shared Values. Of course, the use of charm is a truly magical and fun way to show a potential client your desire to get to know them better and help with their problem. Shared Values can also be developed through similar experiences such as theater, travel, religion and family similarities. Finally, Shared Values are created through reciprocal intentions such as the sharing of information in a deep form of conversation.

Emotional Connectors involve the ability of parties to use emotion to develop strong ties. The attitude of the professional is the most important emotional tie someone can demonstrate with new clients. However, the use of reflection can help build strong ties. The greater the amount of gratitude a professional can show, the stronger the emotional ties that can develop quickly between a professional and a new client.

Credibility and Competence are keys to building immediate trust. Frankly, you need to be world-class or close to it in the competitive professional environment you practice in; clients can spot mediocrity, and the online world will disseminate bad performance in a heartbeat. Another sign of credibility and competence is self-confidence. If you are self-confident, meaning you convey a casual degree of high competence, but not in a bragging manner, this builds credibility with others. Almost as important, a competent professional has great communication skills, meaning they know what to say and what not to say and when to say it or not say it. Technical proficiency without communication proficiency will get you nowhere.

In looking at the circles, the goal is to become great at all three factors: Shared Values, Competency and Confidence, and Emotional Connectors. The intersection of the circles shows the rewards of success in all three factors. Once you become great in the area of Shared Values and Emotional Connectors, that creates a level of mutual attraction among the professional and client that allows the client to become vulnerable and share without filter or reservation their deepest thoughts. That enables the relationship to blossom over a long period of time. Once you become great at Emotional Connectors and Credibility/Competence, both sides easily become willing and active listeners of each other. Listening is perhaps the most important skill in building Insta-Trust. Without listening, your arrogance comes to the forefront, and you lose the ability to impress your new client. Finally, once you become great in Shared Values and Credibility/Competence, you have the ability to transfer your message to your new client. Your client is impressed enough by your demonstrated skill level to be open to your message, but you seal the deal through the use of stories, charm, humor and empathy in a way that takes the client's openness and allows your message to resonate in a manner that helps the client see that you are the right professional to solve their problem.

Once you are able to demonstrate to a potential client that you have developed mutual attraction, are a willing listener and have the ability to transfer a bespoke message or approach that resonates with them in an easy-to-understand manner, you will become an INSTA-TRUST IMPACTOR. You have mastered the first steps to learning how to build Insta-Trust. The rest of this book will give you the specific tools needed to build Insta-Trust.

For your free copy of the WHEELS OF INSTA-TRUST™, please go to www.insta-trust.com.

"GREAT INSTA-TRUST MAKES THE OTHER PERSON FEEL THAT YOU ALWAYS HAVE THEIR OUTCOME AS YOUR NUMBER ONE PRIORITY."

Dr. Larry Jacobson

THE BRIDGE

HIT THEM IN THE HEART LIKE ROBIN HOOD

"Trust is gained by working in others' best interests."
– Inspired by Napoleon Hill

Napoleon Hill was a brilliant man and there is a lot to be said about this quote. Trust is built through working in the other person's best interests, and that is a common theme in this book. If you are not client-centered, not only will you not build trust, your reputation will suffer as one who is self-centered and arrogant.

Let's build on Hill's observation. What is most important is that your client or patient believes in their heart and brain that you are working in their best interest. You can have the best of intentions, but if you cannot make your client or patient truly feel on an emotional level that you are the best person to assist them, you have little opportunity of getting the chance.

Here's a personal example of this… My father employed his best friend as his accountant for many years. His friend was a great guy, but my father's business affairs were becoming quite complex and beyond the scope of his friend. So, with my assistance, my father interviewed new outside CPAs to help him with his accounting, tax and financial affairs. We interviewed at least a half dozen individuals. All had stellar reputations and came off as being technically appropriate for my father's situation. But we had to choose one, and the person we chose got the job based on one simple comment. The winner told my father, "Jack, you can go with many accountants who can do as good a job as I can, and I am pretty damn good. But what you won't get elsewhere is someone who will help you find an auto mechanic if you need one in an emergency pinch. I go to bat for my clients regardless of whether their needs are within the sphere of my competency." That auto mechanic comment resonates with me almost 40 years later. And by the way, to this day, even though my father passed away in 2008 and his accountant is retired, his accountant and I get together every two months for lunch because we enjoy each other's company and I deeply respect his advice on a multitude of subjects. When you are meeting the Patricias of the world who are looking to hire you, make sure that they look at you as more than a technical expert; make them FEEL that you will work in their best interests even if it goes beyond the scope of your narrow specialty.

Around 35 years ago, Milo O. Frank wrote a popular book called *How to Get Your Point Across in 30 Seconds or Less*. Frank strongly believed that you could get your point across in almost any setting in 30 seconds or less and, by inference, build some level of trust. There were many excellent points in his book, including having a compelling hook (more about that in a moment) and personalizing your comments (more about that throughout the book). Frank's advice about getting your point across in 30 seconds might hold weight in meetings with others you already know. However, in most initial professional meetings, you simply cannot build trust in two or three sentences.

In your settings, trust building is conversational, not unidirectional. And that is the flaw of Frank's approach. You need to get their attention quickly, but not at the expense of ignoring what is really important to them on a rational and emotional level. So after your introduction, you need to let them say what the problem is they want you to solve. Let them speak for 30 to 45 seconds, although if they go longer and stay on point, please do not interrupt them. Once you get a decent handle on their problem, before you even ask them follow-up questions regarding the factual nature of the issue, you need to find a way to make a memorable impression on them in terms of how you are professionally and emotionally invested in helping them solve their problem.

In other words, you need to have a grocery bag of hooks that show the new client or patient how committed you are to their success. One size does not fit all; the auto mechanic hook that my father's accountant used might be appropriate for an accountant, but not a surgeon. When developing a hook, keep in mind you are a professional so you do not want to sound phony like a used car salesman. The hook needs to capture their attention in a quick and memorable manner. Here are a few types of hooks that might be helpful.

1. **The success story that paints an irresistible picture.** An oral surgeon might say, "My patients ate apples two weeks after I put in their implants." Or "Because of their new smile, one of my patients interviewed for and got a new job two weeks after my implants." Posit yourself as the Smile Maven. Or an accountant might say, "Anyone can prepare financial statements or tax returns, but I can help your family harmony through getting to know all of you and your family dynamics." In other words, you are the Family Counseling Guru.

2. **How you problem solve in vivid language.** An attorney might tell a new corporate client looking to sell a business that she sits down to plot out an acquisition agreement by drawing a schematic on her iPad. She then can offer to show that client in real time how she might deal with their acquisition on her iPad. In other words, you are the Sketcher Corporate Acquisition Confidant.

3. **How your professional process works in vivid language.** A cosmetic dentist might tell a client how she applies Invisalign solutions to help straighten teeth by explaining not only the steps used, but how the most important thing to her is that patients never need to take anything stronger than Tylenol for pain management. In other words, you are the Painless Dentist.

The point is you need an appropriate hook that is memorable and relevant to their situation. By memorable, I mean a statement or phrase that the other person can remember a day, a week, a month or even a year after meeting you for the first time. The relevance of the hook to their situation is essential; if the hook comes off as canned or inappropriate, you are likely to lose the client or patient right off the bat. Ideally, you should use the hook within the first few minutes of your interaction. In a perfect situation, the hook should be used within the first two minutes after Patricia explains her situation.

A quick point on the use of humor in creating your hook or hook phrase. In many instances, the Patricias of the world are coming to you because they have a serious problem and they are quite anxious about it. The use of humor early on in the conversation would likely be inappropriate, as you might come off as insensitive or egotistical. It is possible that your best approach is to use no humor in your initial trust-building meeting. On the other hand, using a variation of the Lombardi quote above, or using a colorful moniker in describing yourself and your professional approach, can work both as a memorable hook and as a subtle use of humor. When I refer to myself as a "Problem-Solving Maven," it serves to show the Patricias of the world I focus on THEIR problem and it frequently brings a chuckle to their faces.

The purpose of the hook is multidimensional. First, to get their attention by giving them something to remember you. Second, to hit them squarely in the heart and make the decision to hire you based on logic and emotion. A decision to hire you based on their heart and mind is an incredibly strong connection, one that you should always strive to achieve. Third, a great hook works to stimulate further and deeper conversation with the other person. Finally, a great hook will make it much more likely to personalize a nascent relationship. The most enduring and trusting professional relationships are based on a combination of technical excellence and interpersonal stimulation.

"TO BUILD INSTA-TRUST, HIT THEM IN THE HEART. QUICKLY AND MEMORABLY. LIKE ROBIN HOOD."

— Dr. Larry Jacobson

"TRUST BUILDING IS CONVERSATIONAL, NOT UNIDIRECTIONAL."

Dr. Larry Jacobson

"YOU NEED TO GET THEIR ATTENTION QUICKLY, BUT NOT AT THE EXPENSE OF IGNORING WHAT IS REALLY IMPORTANT TO THEM."

Dr. Larry Jacobson

THE 11 PERSONALITY ARCHETYPES YOU WILL NEED TO BUILD INSTA-TRUST WITH

"You take them as you find them."
– Dr. Larry Jacobson

At this point, it is important to discuss 11 different personality archetypes that you might encounter during your initial conversation. Of course, for reasons discussed earlier, your quick default setting should be to assume personality trait number one and then adjust appropriately during the course of your interactions.

1. **THE CLOSE-TO-THE-VEST**—A person who is mysterious about their interests and objectives. An example of a close-to-the-vest Patricia is one who gives out little information about themselves, their concerns or their goals early in the conversation. This type of person is very tight-lipped and you have to be willing to expend a significant amount of time building trust with them before they will open up.

2. **THE TOUGH NUT**—A person who quickly demonstrates a high degree of skepticism about the topics at hand and your ability to help them. An example of a tough nut is a Patricia who not only has a hard time opening up, but also challenges you on your professional questioning approach and knowledge. This type of person may actually be tough or put up a tough persona (you might not know the difference), but you need to expend a significant amount of time on relationship-building questions and then use competence-proving techniques to crack open the nut.

3. **THE KNOW-IT-ALL**—A person who quickly demonstrates they think they know a ton about the topic at hand and/or anything related to the topic, when in reality they don't much at all. This type of person tends

to be argumentative and closed-minded. An example of a know-it-all is someone who aggressively expresses through words and actions that they are an equal, if not superior, to the professional with respect to the technical matters at hand. You deal with this type of person, not by being competitive or arrogant about your knowledge base, but by showing quiet competence regarding the matter at hand and being confident in your interactions with them.

4. **THE NOVICE**—A person who quickly demonstrates little or no knowledge about the topic at hand, and knows it. An example of this type of person is someone who knows they don't know much about the matter they are discussing with you. They require a great deal of education, and you need to be patient with the novice since they are likely not only to have a knowledge gap, but also a comfort gap, both of which need to be addressed.

5. **THE TIRE KICKER**—A person who quickly demonstrates little or no interest in the topic at hand. An example of this type of person is someone who likes to waste your time; they are unfocused and frequently insincere. When you deal with a tire kicker, you should ask questions to determine the seriousness of their situation and the urgency of their needs.

6. **THE INDECISIVE**—A person who quickly demonstrates a lack of focus or ability to make even the most basic decisions. An example of this type of person is someone who asks a lot of questions and initially seems interested in a professional relationship, but then when the time comes to make a decision on hiring you, they delay by coming up with questionable excuses. When you deal with an indecisive, you should gently press them as to whether they have any questions. Once they are done asking questions, the best approach is to politely but firmly ask if they are ready to commit to a professional relationship.

7. **THE LONG-TIMER**—A person who quickly demonstrates a deliberate and potentially lengthy approach to making decisions related to the topic at hand and to the relationship between the parties. An example of a long-timer is someone whose personality is not one of indecision but one of deliberation. A long-timer has a genuine need for a professional relationship and in fact wants a long-term relationship; you can distinguish the indecisive from the long-timer by ascertaining whether Patricia has an uncertain personality (meaning indecisive) or is someone who is deliberate but really looking for a long-term relationship.

8. **THE SCHMOOZER**—A person who quickly demonstrates more of a need to socialize than to address the topic at hand. An example is someone who comes into your office and spends an inordinate amount of time talking on matters that are totally irrelevant. A schmoozer might also be a tire kicker or an indecisive. But with a schmoozer, you need to take control of the conversation in a gentle way and let them know that you are there to help them by moving to important matters.

9. **THE KNOWLEDGEABLE**—A person who quickly and clearly demonstrates a high level of understanding of the topic at hand. An example of this is a general counsel at a company who is interacting with an outside counsel at a law firm on a matter where the general counsel already has a high knowledge base. You should respect the expertise of the knowledgeable and in fact should dedicate early efforts to building the relationship, showing empathy for the other person and their situation and, when getting into the advice stage, speak with the other as a true equal.

10. **THE QUICK DRAW**—A person who demonstrates a desire to get to the resolution of the matters fast, regardless of their knowledge base. An example of this type of person is someone who comes into your office and says, "I have 20 minutes. Tell me what I need to know before I decide to hire you." In this situation, acknowledge their time constraints, but explain you have a process to get to know them and their problem. If you go over the time they allot, gently explain it is in both of your best interests to continue the conversation.

11. **THE EGOMANIAC**—A person who quickly and clearly demonstrates as their top priority a need to feel superior to the professional on the matter at hand and wants to dominate the relationship from an interpersonal perspective. This type of person is easy to discern within the first 30 seconds of an interaction. They're egotistical, arrogant and come off as poor listeners even when with skilled professionals. Since they are used to being told by others what they want to hear rather than what they need to hear, you must quickly display high competence and quiet confidence with the egomaniac by both taking over the conversation and acknowledging the ego in the person that they are dealing with.

Keeping in mind that building quick trust is the desired outcome of initial interactions with prospective clients, patients or negotiating counterparties, your initial posture should be to treat them as a true unknown quantity. After the initial interactions show the client falls into one or more of the ten other archetypes, then you can start the trust-building process in earnest. There are no simple answers as to the best way to deal with each of these archetypes. There is a simple approach that applies to all situations and personalities. That approach involves your having an educational and inquisitive technique with prospective clients. By engaging in that approach, you should ascertain the timeframe and commitment of the prospective client. In doing so, you need to exhibit substantial patience in interacting. Whether dealing with such archetypes as the novice, the know-it-all, the tire kicker or the long-timer, it takes time to build trust with people that truly are not matter-of-fact in terms of intention or action. Impatience can be the death of professional trust building. You know more about the matter at hand than the potential client. Don't ruin a potentially beneficial relationship by demonstrating impatience when dealing with a client who is challenging, impetuous or deliberate.

You would love to deal with clients that you can quickly ascertain are either knowledgeable about the subject matter at hand and/or are decisive in their decision making. It appears easy to build trust with those types of clients or patients because you can eliminate time needed to express competence and move more quickly to building a collaborative relationship and entering problem-solving mode. That may or may not be true; some knowledgeable or decisive clients can be slow to warm up to you.

Alas, you don't get to choose all of your clients. Even so-called knowledgeable or decisive clients might be involved in a situation where they are less knowledgeable or sure of themselves than usual. Thus, you need to keep your antenna up in terms of how to build trust even if it appears on the surface that trust building can be accomplished quickly.

"IMPATIENCE CAN BE THE DEATH OF PROFESSIONAL TRUST BUILDING."

Dr. Larry Jacobson

One critical point in terms of the archetypes is that every individual you deal with is, even to a limited degree, an egomaniac. Some show it in the first 30 seconds of an interaction and others for whom egomania is not the dominant trait might show it in more subtle ways. Regardless, everyone has a mindset where they are the center of their own universe and they get to decide whom they invite in to play. When you are interacting with anyone who exhibits one or more of the other ten archetypes, please keep in the back of your mind that there is at least a little egomaniac in everyone and don't ever get so cocky to think you can come off as superior to any potential patient, client or negotiating counterparty.

REMEMBER THE BEST WAY TO DEAL WITH PEOPLE WITH ANY KIND OF EGO IS TO LET THEM KNOW YOUR NUMBER ONE PRIORITY IS TO MAKE THEM LOOK AND FEEL GOOD.

In summary, your goal is to treat trust building as your number one outcome in terms of a business objective. If you build trust, the professional outcome shall come. Trust building depends on the different personalities of the potential clients and patients you meet. Your global approach is the same regardless of the personality type; you should go into every interaction with an open mind. Then you should move on to ascertaining the personality archetype of the other person and figure out how to find ways to build trust, educating them in a collaborative and problem-solving manner. Because at the end of the day, you take your clients as you find them. You aren't a social worker, psychologist or psychiatrist. You need to build trust based on who they are and not whom you wish them to be.

Ask Yourself

QUESTION ONE: Do I appear to the potential client or counterparty that I am more focused on my interests or their interests?

QUESTION TWO: How do I demonstrate to the potential client or counterparty that I am most concerned about *their* interests?

QUESTION THREE: Do I prioritize trust building over short-term profits?

QUESTION FOUR: Do I monitor my reputation and do I consider acting in a trusting manner as my professional lodestar?

QUESTION FIVE: Do I start my professional interactions with a potential client or patient from the perspective of nonjudgment and lack of bias?

QUESTION SIX: Do I attempt to ascertain the personality archetype of the other person and then adjust my trust-building approach to the personality of the other person?

QUESTION SEVEN: Am I patient enough to take as much time as is necessary to build a trusting relationship with the other person?

"THE SECRET OF INSTA-TRUST IS IT SETS THE GROUNDWORK, THE FRAMEWORK AND THE TRUST WORK TO GO FROM INSTA- TO LONG-TERM TRUST."

Dr. Larry Jacobson

|03|

HOW TRUST IS EARNED
IN THE FIRST FIVE MINUTES

"For the great doesn't happen through impulse alone, and is a succession of little things that are brought together."
–Vincent van Gogh

Trust cannot be bought or sold. Trust cannot be procured through advertising or social media activity. Yes, excellent reputations can be enhanced through referrals, social media and recommendations. But trust and trusting reputations are built through hard work and interpersonal interactions with hundreds, if not thousands, of individuals. One-on-one trust can take one minute, five minutes, an hour, a day, a week, a month, a year or longer to develop. In the virtual world and in many new client interactions, quick trust is the objective. I call the development of quick trust in an initial interaction Insta-Trust.

What is Insta-Trust? Insta-Trust is a process where strong trust is developed between a professional and a new patient, client, or negotiating counterparty in a virtual or in-person setting within one hour of the start of the interaction.

There are four key elements to Insta-Trust:

1. Relationship building,
2. A meeting setting,
3. Establishing a quietly confident persona, and
4. Speed.

"THE GOAL OF INSTA-TRUST IS TO EARN TRUST QUICKLY IN ORDER TO PROVIDE A CLIENT OR PATIENT WITH THE PROFESSIONAL SERVICE THAT IS IN THEIR BEST INTEREST."

Dr. Larry Jacobson

Before getting into the components of how one develops an Insta-Trust mindset, let's delve into how trust is developed generally. Remember that in an initial meeting, the other side cannot observe your integrity. While they might have read some online reviews or other social media chatter about you, the reality is that once you start a conversation with another person, all they really have to go on in making a trust assessment is how you conduct yourself during that initial call, email exchange or video chat. I cannot emphasize more strongly how vital your presence, even if you cannot be physically seen, is in making a quick impression on a prospective business contact. This starts with having a quiet confidence persona. If you do not come across as self-assured, why would anyone trust you to perform surgery on them, negotiate a big deal or provide sophisticated legal advice?

Step one is having a quiet confidence persona that you are the right person for the job; and frankly, if you are not the right person for the job, your best option is to tell the other person you are not the right person to work with and give them several referrals as to who can best help them. All too often I have seen professionals take on matters in which they have little or no training. Oftentimes those situations result in unsatisfactory endings. I turn down over 70 percent of prospective clients who call me because I cannot help them achieve their professional objectives. Sometimes those individuals get angry at me and end the conversation quickly. But most of those individuals are very thankful for my candor. If we get that far, I spend quite a bit of time with those individuals, without requiring compensation, giving them personalized advice as to how best to wind down their oral surgery practices. They are grateful for the advice, and on more than one occasion, oral surgeons whose practices I decided not to represent have referred me to clients whom I could successfully represent. In your situation, even when it is apparent that you might not be able to assist a Patricia with respect to their specific situation, please find a way to help them either by giving advice as to alternative solutions not involving you or giving them a strong referral to someone who can assist them.

Thus, putting aside the Insta-Trust process, one of the most important things you can do to build immediate trust (after developing a natural quiet confidence persona) is to develop a candid approach (the mindset is described in the next paragraph) toward the people you interact with. In professional settings, prospective clients and patients like to work with straight shooters. All too often you interact with professionals who hem and haw in terms of their advice. They talk about, "Maybe this might happen or maybe that might happen." I get it to a degree; I am an attorney and understand that malpractice cases can hinge on proper and full disclosure of risks with respect to a particular procedure or case. Yet there is a way to properly inform a prospective client or patient of the risks involved while still conveying an honest assessment of the situation. If the situation is dire or has a low chance of success, the best approach is to be candid about it and do it in a manner that shows empathy and to say that if hired, you will do your absolute best to help the client or patient. That is a far more ethical approach than coming across like a gunslinger and telling the client or patient that you are going to get them through the situation successfully. On the other hand, if the situation is murky, with a good but uncertain chance of success, then the best approach is to be upfront about the probabilities and then quickly give several approaches that you have already thought about as increasing the probability of success. A professional who can quickly and competently come up with multiple potential options in discussing a murky situation with a potential client or patient in an initial meeting comes across as confident, skilled, empathic, collaborative and, most importantly, as someone people want to work with.

Even in situations where a certain result is probable or highly likely, the trustworthy professional constantly acts from a position of compassionate candor. Compassionate candor means always telling the truth to a client or patient and doing it in a manner that acknowledges their goals, their personality and their fears. A "tell it like it is" approach, without a strong bedside manner, rarely conveys a level of strong trust. I learned this lesson the hard way as a younger attorney. I always thought that clients, especially sophisticated clients, wanted to deal with straight shooters who did not sugarcoat their advice. Some do, but the reality is, many clients want their confident advisors to give a more polished explanation of the matter at hand, potential options and recommended approaches. You can never go wrong if you quickly and professionally present a client with your thoughts (after giving them an opportunity to lay out their concerns and objectives) with empathy. That is compassionate candor.

A wise mentor told me early in my career that you really don't know if you are on the road to a trusting relationship until you are confronted by a client who says something that is either factually erroneous, exhibits a level of stubbornness that indicates doubt as to whether they will take you seriously or refuses to listen to anything you have to say. Our natural inclination is to politely (and occasionally not so politely) tell the other person to take a hike. Isn't life too short to work with people whose first impression in an initial trust-building interaction is one of negativity or stupidity? Sometimes, but life is more interesting if you can use your best efforts to find a way to get through to challenging people. Sometimes challenging people can become some of your most rewarding patients or clients once you break through their armor. So how do you break through?

"LIFE IS MORE INTERESTING IF YOU CAN USE YOUR BEST EFFORTS TO FIND A WAY TO GET THROUGH TO CHALLENGING PEOPLE."

– Dr. Larry Jacobson

While you may be the subject matter expert and comfortable speaking about your expertise, the person on the receiving end is often anxious. Thus, it should be anticipated that in many situations, as a skilled professional, you are going to be trying to build Insta-Trust with people who come across as very challenging. Many of those challenging individuals are going to give cues that they are not taking what you are saying seriously.

Your seat-of-the-pants reaction to a challenging person is to put up a "superiority" persona and tell them they should simply "trust me." Such an approach is the absolute worst thing you can do.

You need to build an INSTA-TRUST persona. An Insta-Trust persona is a mindset that requires you to always focus first on trust building with the person you are interacting with. Don't show you are the smart one. Show you are the helpful one. Your mindset must be CLIENT-CENTRIC. A client-centric professional can display their technical genius in subtle ways once they establish Insta-Trust.

When faced with a client or patient who appears to be disregarding what you are saying or even ignoring it, your approach must be to remain calm and continue to ask questions (even in the face of continuing anxiety or anger) that are designed to get the person to a stage where they begin to face the reality of the situation. In other words, the first part of the process is to get the other person into a psychological state where they are getting as calm as possible. You can ask questions such as "Why are you feeling this way?," "Can I do a better job of explaining the situation and solutions?," "What facts can I give you that will help you understand what we are discussing?" and "I have as long as you need to answer your questions; what are your three top concerns and objectives for us to work on together?"

"THE TWO WORST WORDS YOU CAN EVER SAY TO A CLIENT: 'TRUST ME.' THAT WILL PUT UP A SHIELD IN THEIR MIND THAT WILL NEVER COME DOWN."

Dr. Larry Jacobson

The relationship-building process is designed to achieve a few goals. First, to show the other person that you truly care about them as a person. Second, to show that you acknowledge their concerns, whether factual, emotional or situational. A cancer patient, a patient with a painful wisdom tooth, a client acquiring a business or a client under an IRS audit all have a multitude of real and emotional concerns about the matter at hand. Third, to show via questioning and empathy that you truly have the technical expertise to help them. Finally, and most importantly, you are conveying that you have a collaborative approach toward problem solving and that you and Patricia are in it together to get the problem addressed in a successful manner.

The next step beyond the question phase designed to calm down the nervous or insensitive Patricia is to begin to explain in a matter-of-fact manner your technical assessment of the situation and how you propose to solve it. Insta-Trust requires the professional who is being asked to perform a very important skill for Patricia to be highly competent in their field. An incompetent or minimally competent professional that is out of their depth on a particular matter not only will develop a relationship of distrust with potential clients, but will violate the number one precept that all medical and dental students learn: DO NO HARM. This precept applies equally to attorneys, CPAs and other professionals. All too often, professionals are asked to perform services on a matter in which they have little or no competence. And for reasons of finance or ego, these professionals engage in activities in which they have little training or experience. These professionals engage in a manner that disrespects the people they serve and shows a high level of distrust. Therefore, in order to build fast trust, you better know your stuff or the other person will likely see through your façade. In the event they don't see through it immediately, an imposter skill level will eventually be exposed and you will find it very difficult to restore reputation and a trustworthy persona.

If necessary, let Patricia vent and show you are paying attention by staying silent and taking notes. Then, using quiet confidence to demonstrate your competence in the matter at hand, move the conversation to the point of discussing options and solutions. The obvious approach taken by most professionals is to simply lay out options and then select the one they think is in the best interest of the client. This approach might work with the impatient patient/client or the novice. But in most situations, the obvious approach is amateurish. The far better approach with respect to each option is to ask the patient/client if they understand what is being suggested. Encourage questions. Make sure they understand what you are saying. If not, repeat. Do this with respect to every option. Then ask if they have any questions regarding all of the options. Once you are satisfied that all of the options have been thoroughly understood and vetted, then ask if they are ready to discuss the best option for them.

From a trust-building standpoint, professional recommendations are the fork in the road in which trust can be gained or lost. In making a recommendation, you need to be firm in your own mind that it is the right approach for the patient/client. As discussed later in more depth, the recommendation must always put the client's interests first. All too often, professionals see dollar signs as their primary motivation. Sometimes you put your ego first and do not clinically assess the real costs, benefits and probabilities of your recommended solution. Sometimes you use Patricia's emotional state as a guiding factor in making your recommendations. While the other person's emotional state is something that should be taken into account when making professional recommendations, it should not be the dominant factor. Recommendations should always be based on what is likely to result in the best possible outcome for the patient/client. As such, recommendations should be explained in terms that the patient/client understands. You should ask the patient/client if they have any questions or concerns about the recommendation.

Now from an Insta-Trust standpoint, here comes the critical part. Few things in professional practice are black and white in terms of optimal solutions or come with absolutely no risk. And not all recommendations come with a very high level of confidence in a positive result. In recommending a specific approach, the professional needs to decide how best to break news that might or might not always have a happy ending. In making recommendations, the professional should calmly assess the range of probabilities of the recommendation's potential success. A recommendation should never contain a precise percentage of success. First, none of us are computers who are so absolutely sure of our capabilities that we can predict our success with precision. Experience tells us there may be facts about the situation that are not disclosed to us or won't be known to us until we are hired and start work. Second, by giving the probability of success in terms of a reasonable range, you show clients and patients a level of competence based on experience while acknowledging from their perspective the ambiguity of certain situations. When the probability of success is high, you should acknowledge that in strong terms and not dwell on very low-risk probabilities (attorneys are particularly focused on discussing the probability of events with a low level of probability). You should mention the possibility of low-probability events, but not fixate on them. In fact, that approach should guide the professional discussion of risk and probabilities; they should be discussed in a calm and clinical manner.

Once the risks are laid out, you need to go into active listening mode to assess whether the patient/client understands the risk assessment. Again, patience must be exhibited. First, this is only a preliminary meeting and the assessment might change if you are hired. Second, the patient/client might continue to show anxiety and have a need to discuss risks more thoroughly in order to process the given advice. Third, the risk assessment discussion frequently results in the patient/client disclosing additional facts that are relevant to a potential reassessment of the situation. Conversely, the risk assessment discussion can sometimes stir you to look for more evidence to either support or disprove your recommendation. In any event, in Insta-Trust discussions, nothing should be taken for granted because the situation is only being explored in preliminary terms; the nature of the preliminary analysis is a function of the completeness of the information available to you in the initial meeting.

Here are the two most important parts of the nascent professional relationship and Insta-Trust. First, your main objective is to build a personal relationship with Patricia. All the prior discussion of technical matters, options and risks are being done on a preliminary basis. Real facts can and do change under the sharp light of a cool and lengthy analysis.

You need to come across as:

1. Quietly competent,

2. Knowledgeable,

3. Willing to ask and be asked important (and sometimes unimportant) questions about the matter,

4. Showing a true interest in the other person, and

5. Making it clear that you are only developing a potential solution to their problem.

Thus, the Insta-Trust approach uses high competence as a process to bond on a personal level. Remember, RELATIONSHIP BUILDING PRECEDES THE HARD DISCUSSION OF THE CLIENT'S REAL PROBLEM.

There is no shame in me or you admitting when we are not the most appropriate professional for a particular client. An experienced professional can sense if they can establish a relationship with a client that can result in an optimal solution. You don't have to love your clients or even like them in their entirety. However, to build a trusting relationship, you need to feel you can be of assistance to them and that in turn they are willing to commit fully to a process where candor is essential. If after substantial effort, your Insta-Trust process does not reveal the other person to be someone you feel comfortable will be a true partner in addressing the matter at hand, you should decline the representation. No amount of money is worth working with a person who demonstrates a lack of commitment to a process that will require you to spend significant time and resources.

WHEELS OF INSTA-TRUST™:
Shared Values

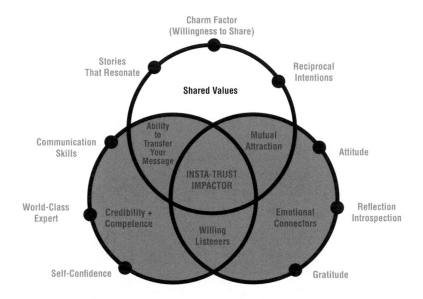

The Shared Values concept in the WHEELS OF INSTA-TRUST™ applies to the ideas described in this chapter. When you develop Shared Values, you do so by engaging in the three key techniques of using stories that resonate, demonstrating a willingness to share with your Patricia and exchanging reciprocal intentions. When you use stories to build your relationship, you demonstrate a form of quiet confidence that resonates with the other person. When you demonstrate a willingness to be compassionately candid with the other person, you express a form of vulnerability that makes it much more likely that you will build a relationship and get hired. When you and the other person demonstrate reciprocal intentions of being candid, emotionally available and sharing information, you are reaching the pinnacle of Shared Values since you are developing an emotional bond that will allow both of you to go to the next level of building a relationship and a professional work engagement.

The relationship building part is the key ingredient to the commencement of a successful professional relationship.

Ask Yourself

QUESTION ONE: What are the components of my quiet confidence persona?

QUESTION TWO: Am I compassionately candid with Patricia?

QUESTION THREE: Am I patient enough to allow Patricia to express her frustrations, anxieties and concerns about the problem and solution, and her feelings about working with me?

QUESTION FOUR: How good are my risk assessment skills and how skilled am I in explaining the risks of the matters without coming off as overly dramatic?

QUESTION FIVE: Do I encourage questions and conversations during the discussion part of the Insta-Trust process?

QUESTION SIX: Do I exhibit quiet confidence in my preliminary recommendation?

QUESTION SEVEN: Do I focus on building the relationship first and fast, and then acknowledge that the fact-finding part of the process just might be the beginning of a longer analysis?

BONUS QUESTION: Do I believe I have gained trust?

"YOU CAN MASTER THE SKILLS OF COMMUNICATION, EXHIBIT THE BEST FORM OF QUIET CONFIDENCE AND WORK EFFICIENTLY, BUT IF YOU DON'T BUILD THE RELATIONSHIP FIRST, THERE IS NO INSTA-TRUST."

Dr. Larry Jacobson

04

THE BULLSHIT METERS ARE ALWAYS RUNNING IN BOTH DIRECTIONS

Truth is a messy thing. There are certain matters where truth is not in doubt. The earth is round. Cigarette smoking kills. The Yankees have won more World Series than any Major League Baseball team. Yet in the vast majority of issues that are faced in the real world, there is no absolute assurance. If we learned anything in 2020 and 2021, it is that the future is highly speculative and predictions and risk assessments are just that. We live in a world where the past is not as indicative of the future as we think.

When do you sense that someone is bullshitting you? For that matter, what exactly is bullshit for the purposes of trust assessment? Is simple puffing bullshit? Is it bullshit if a person takes a view that is far more likely than not to be false but cannot be entirely ruled out of the reasonableness spectrum? For the purposes of this book, how quickly can you assess a bullshit artist and what should your response be in the event that you discover you are being bullshitted?

These are not easy questions and there are no easy answers. But let's start with the definition of bullshit in an Insta-Trust situation. Bullshit is a statement or course of conduct that is (1) almost certainly false, (2) designed completely to enhance the likelihood of the other person to engage in behavior that is far more heavily advantaged to the bullshitter than it is to the person hearing or observing the bullshit and (3) intended to take advantage of a perceived information gap between the bullshitter and the recipient. Let's take each of these concepts one at a time.

When someone is engaging in bullshit, he or she is almost always exaggerating to a degree that is blatantly unreasonable. Bullshit is not puffing, it is not being "salesy," it is not portraying a gray area situation in the most favorable light for the bullshitter. No, bullshit is the use of words in a manner that is not believable when examined carefully. A bullshitter might say that there is a high degree of risk of death if a man undergoes a vasectomy. In fact, the risk of death in such a medical procedure is infinitesimal, probably one in ten million. A bullshitter might say that the polio vaccine can cause serious side effects, even though there is no scientific evidence that suggests such an outcome. A bullshitter might tell you that you look like George Clooney, even if you weigh 300 pounds and are bald.

In other words, bullshit is used to greatly exaggerate a fact or opinion to such an extent that if you asked 100 people who are knowledgeable on the matter of the bullshit, at least 99 people would call out the bullshitter. Bullshit is exaggeration on steroids; it does not involve matters where there could be an honest difference of assessment of fact or opinion.

Bullshit is designed to enhance the likelihood of the other person to engage in behavior that is far more advantageous to the bullshitter than it is to the person hearing or observing the bullshit. Bullshit is not a casual statement or a casual attempt to get someone to do something. Bullshit is generally not used on unimportant matters; bullshit is a deliberate attempt by someone to convey something of importance to the other person. In addition, the bullshit is expressly designed to work to the substantial advantage of the bullshitter. For example, if a dentist who has never removed an impacted wisdom tooth tells a prospective patient that he has removed 50 impacted wisdom teeth, the statement is not only factually false, but it is expressly designed to impress the patient about his or her capabilities to his or her financial advantage. A CPA who has never worked on international tax matters who tells a client that she has substantial experience in such matters is a bullshitter because the CPA is asking the client to trust her ability to help on a complicated tax matter in which he or she is a novice. The bullshitter smells blood because he or she senses the potential client is insecure about the matter being brought to the professional.

"BULLSHIT IS DESIGNED TO ENHANCE THE LIKELIHOOD OF THE OTHER PERSON TO ENGAGE IN BEHAVIOR THAT IS FAR MORE ADVANTAGEOUS TO THE BULLSHITTER THAN IT IS TO THE PERSON HEARING OR OBSERVING THE BULLSHIT."

Dr. Larry Jacobson

Finally, the bullshitter attempts to take advantage of a perceived information gap between the bullshitter and the recipient. If the bullshitter senses the potential client is knowledgeable about the subject matter being discussed, they will make a risk assessment that it may not be worth using a bullshit technique. But if the potential client is seriously lacking in knowledge about the matter at hand, the unethical professional frequently uses the information gap to spout bullshit about their background or expertise. Using my example of the CPA with no international tax expertise, she might throw out some key phrases like transfer pricing, Subpart F and tax havens to try to convince the potential client that he or she has a deep background in the area, when in fact, the CPA wouldn't know about transfer pricing, Subpart F or a tax haven issue if her life literally depended on it.

The challenge is that early in the stages of a professional relationship, it might be very difficult for the potential client to identify bullshit when they hear it or see it. This is especially true if the first interaction is by phone, where the client cannot see facial expressions and might have a hard time assessing voice tone. Moreover, this is true where the potential client has a very limited knowledge base regarding the matter being discussed. I am an attorney and a CPA by training; I can sense bullshit on corporate and tax matters, but I would be clueless in knowing if I was being bullshitted by a trademark attorney or an accountant whose specialty is internal controls or fraud detection. If I see an endodontist to have a root canal procedure, I have no idea if I am being bullshitted about the procedure or the pain of the procedure. The information gap should help the potential client recognize that a professional who casually throws out highly technical terms in order to impress might, on the one hand, be a mere egotist (but highly skilled) or, on the other, someone unsuitable to work on their matter. In either case, the use of highly technical language by an expert very early in an Insta-Trust interaction should make the potential client wary. Step one in determining a potential bullshit artist is the use of technical jargon early in the interaction. Ethical professionals rarely engage in such behavior.

Step two in determining a potential bullshit artist is the speed in which the professional wants to press the client to hire him or her. On balance, bullshit artists are not patient people. They want to "close the deal" quickly. While bullshit artists might appear to be building rapport with the other person, their questions tend to be of the type not to discover and assuage the true concerns of the client, but rather the superficial rapport building is designed to move to being hired quickly and at a significant financial advantage to the professional.

Step three in determining a potential bullshit artist is detecting/noticing someone who expresses early concern about something that is totally irrelevant to the matter at hand. A competent oral surgeon is not going to ask you about your children in an initial discussion about a dental implant. A competent ethical attorney is not going to ask you about whether you are a Yankee or Red Sox fan in an initial discussion about a corporate acquisition unless it is a video chat and someone has a visible picture of memorabilia of one of the teams. Deceptive individuals frequently appear to work overly hard to build rapport on matters that are "suck up" in nature.

Finally, step four in determining a potential bullshit artist is noticing when someone brings up the financial aspect of representation far earlier than is generally appropriate. If you bring up fee schedules unprompted and well before the conclusion of a discussion of the actual professional matter, you are showing a lack of empathy. More crucially, the introduction of financial matters prematurely can be a sign that you are not quite as experienced or polished as you are trying to present yourself as being.

Now the demonstration of one or more of these four behaviors is not automatically associated with bullshit. A limited knowledge base on the part of the client and your use of jargon could be a sign of insecurity on your part. Sometimes a "cutting to the chase" attitude could be because the professional is busy with other matters or preoccupied with a personal situation. An expression of an inappropriate social comment can result from a professional being socially awkward or inexperienced in small talk. Finally, the premature introduction of financial aspects of representation can sometimes occur when a professional is under severe financial pressure or pressure from a partner to bring in more business. However, none of these behaviors are appropriate in terms of building Insta-Trust.

So if bullshit is hard to detect, why discuss it here? Your potential client's antenna will be up from the very beginning. Some might be of a very trusting type, but many potential clients are likely to have had bad prior experiences with other professionals and businesses.

"THE ETHICAL PROFESSIONAL MAKES A CONSCIOUS EFFORT TO UNDERSTAND HOW A BULLSHIT ARTIST MIGHT BE PORTRAYED AND WORKS HARD NOT TO COME OFF AS A BULLSHIT ARTIST."

– Dr. Larry Jacobson

Remember, reputation matters in our era of social media, Yelp and Google reviews. You might be the most conscientious professional, but if your approach is viewed by enough potential clients as being bullshitty, your actual character may not be relevant.

The purpose of this discussion is to reinforce your need to be continuously introspective about your new client relationship-building skills. This is built on in the Interlude part of this book. You take continuing education courses to maintain and enhance your technical skills. You should care just as deeply that the world of clients and potential clients view you as someone who is highly skilled AND highly caring about your clients, their problems and tailored solutions to their problems. A perceived bullshit artist appears to deeply care more about themselves than their clients or patients. You do not want to be perceived as a bullshit artist. That perception will be a serious impediment to building Insta-Trust. Insta-Trust professionals deliberately discard bullshitting behaviors that can be perceived as offensive, self-absorbed and self-centered.

Ask Yourself

QUESTION ONE: How quickly can someone assess a bullshit artist and how confident can someone be when they are being bullshitted?

QUESTION TWO: What is the difference between bullshitting and demonstrating professional confidence?

QUESTION THREE: How do I handle the knowledge gap between myself and my patient/client in terms of jargon and tone?

QUESTION FOUR: Am I coming off as too self-absorbed and concerned about my status as opposed to my patient's or client's concerns?

QUESTION FIVE: Am I coming across as trying to end the professional conversation too quickly?

QUESTION SIX: Am I raising the financial aspects of a professional relationship too early in the discussion?

QUESTION SEVEN: Am I constantly evaluating how I am coming across to potential clients or patients to avoid being perceived as a potential bullshitter?

"MUTUAL ATTRACTION IS BUILT WHEN YOU ANTICIPATE AND ADDRESS THE VULNERABILITY OF THE OTHER SIDE."

Dr. Larry Jacobson

05

TRUST ATTRIBUTES: THE GOOD, THE BAD AND THE REALLY UGLY

Is trust really necessary for you to conduct all aspects of a professional assignment or is it more of a "nice to have" attribute?

Keep in mind that trust is a very difficult concept to define on many different levels. The term is used within different contexts; yet most of the aspects of trust are difficult to put into words. It can also have different meanings within different settings. An oncologist may use one type of process to build trust when explaining how to combat and treat a specific type of cancer and use a totally different process to build trust when dealing with a different type of cancer. Context matters in trust building. Moreover, can you really measure trust, either in a qualitative or quantitative manner?

Research indicates that trust has been analyzed from two different perspectives. The first is a behavioral perspective, meaning that trust is viewed as a behavior within a relationship in which the individuals are viewed as making decisions primarily from a rational lens. The second perspective analyzes trust from a psychological perspective, meaning trust is a behavior that focuses more on the state of mind of those in the relationship, regardless of the rational nature they might possess. Let's look at each perspective separately.

Many academics' view of trust is that individuals are rational actors who observe the actions of others and analyze whether the other person or persons are trustworthy, based on the assumption that the other person is making rational choices as to whether to engage in trusting or deceitful behavior. On the other hand, classic economic theory is based on the assumption that businesspeople (including professionals) will act in a profit-maximizing manner. Yet, self-interest can manifest itself in either a cooperative or competitive manner. Research studies have shown that when an individual has a noticeably cooperative disposition, the result is more often that the individual will develop trust and a satisfactory outcome (in negotiation settings and elsewhere), whereas if the individual has a demonstrably competitive disposition, a satisfactory outcome of gain or professional results is less likely. Other studies have shown that cooperative behavior in a negotiation setting will produce an initially trusting relationship, even when communication between the parties is limited. Conversely, competitive behavior (meaning that one or both parties act strictly in a manner designed to benefit their side) tends to result in a suspicious or non-trusting relationship.

The key element regarding trust has been mentioned previously but bears repeating at this stage. Trust develops or doesn't develop because of the uncertainty caused by two or more individuals meeting for the first time on a matter of significance to at least one side. The matters that you are being asked to work on have significant importance to the other person. They might need estate planning, a knee replacement, a root canal, assistance in negotiating the sale of a house or a piece of real estate or drawing up plans for a new building. The point is that even when the parties are more rational than not, there is a huge anxiety gap between the parties, with you likely having and exhibiting little anxiety and with Patricia exhibiting anxiety to a different degree.

That anxiety gap manifests itself in the psychological aspects of trust. Since individuals are not robots who act in a purely rational manner 100 percent of the time, there is a significant psychological dimension to trust building. Even professionals do not act rationally all the time; your actions can be motivated by other work concerns, family matters and other extraneous issues. From a psychological standpoint, trust involves (1) vulnerability, (2) one or both parties must have something of importance to lose if the other party acts in a deceptive, self-serving or incompetent manner, and (3) the less knowledgeable party has little or no information regarding the trustworthiness of the other party.

Let's explore all three important aspects of trust.

First, vulnerability. The person who is coming to you, even if they are highly skilled (say a general counsel of a large company asking for legal assistance on a complex legal matter), has a level of vulnerability when interviewing new representation. In this example, the general counsel is under substantial pressure to find the most appropriate legal representation to get the matter handled satisfactorily and at a reasonable cost. The general counsel's vulnerability might not be due to subject matter knowledge, but in the concern of being viewed by her superior as hiring the right law firm to handle the matter. In most cases, Patricia is not a knowledgeable general counsel type and has limited knowledge regarding the matter at hand, so the vulnerability level is quite high. These persons truly fall into the category of not knowing what they don't know. They might be scared, nervous or mildly anxious. When you intend to build Insta-Trust, you need to acknowledge the other side's vulnerability and work hard to show the other person that you understand their concerns and will work collaboratively to achieve the best possible result. Remember, Patricia has little or no opportunity to observe how you are doing on her matter until well into the relationship. The lack of monitoring is a key component of the professional relationship, so during the first five minutes of an initial meeting with Patricia, you should have a mindset of anticipating and addressing the vulnerability of the other side. The goal should be to get the potential client to feel comfortable that you will not take advantage where there is no ability to take note of his or her behavior.

Second, the importance of the matter from a trust-building standpoint. The importance of the matter impacts both sides of the professional relationship. From your perspective, pride in doing great work not only provides a huge psychological boost, but should result in long-term financial rewards and stability. From the client's perspective, the matter could literally be life or death, financial prosperity or ruin, or a long-term personal benefit or a personal calamity. From the client's perspective, any matter in which they are looking for professional assistance is a very big deal. Thus, the professional must quickly acknowledge the importance of the matter early in the Insta-Trust meeting and be prepared to spend as much time as necessary explaining the issue to the potential client and demonstrating a high level of empathy for their anxiety.

Third, the information gap and how it impacts Insta-Trust building. Think of a situation where you had complete and absolute knowledge about a particular situation and your spouse or close friend had zero knowledge about either the matter or how to evaluate the matter. For example, assume you needed to ask your spouse or close friend for funds to invest with you in a piece of commercial property. What do you do? Do you jump in and say you found a great investment opportunity and let's invest? Or do you view this as a multi-step process where you lay out everything and leave the ask for later. In this example, what I would do is start by saying, "I have been spending significant time looking at real estate opportunities, and I have been working with several competent real estate professionals in my search." I would show that I have been spending significant time investing in educating myself as to how to evaluate real estate opportunities. I would bring in one or more of my professionals to explain the opportunity. I would explain the potential risks and rewards of the investment. I would spend a huge amount of time anticipating and answering their questions on a matter that came out of the clear blue sky. In fact, I wouldn't even ask them to make a decision in the first meeting. Maybe not even the second meeting either. Beyond all of this, I would not make the proposed investment so large that failure would ruin their finances or my friendship. Second, I wouldn't make the ask until each and every question, concern or information gap is addressed. This exercise shows that where there is a huge information gap between the parties, you need to be prepared to spend an inordinate amount of time investigating the factual context and then explaining the relevance of important facts before getting to their opinions regarding the resolution of the matter.

So is trust more of a rational or psychological process? The attorney in me would like to think that you and I are rational actors and that psychological concerns are of little importance. However, experience tells me that even when you or I are dealing with the most purported rational actors, i.e., scientists, economists, physicians or attorneys, the psychological aspects of trust building can trump the rational aspects. Even among so-called professional-to-professional relationships, trust-building processes are as important as the perceived competence of the other person. Because even in high-level relationships, if the first party does not believe the second party will deliver on a timely basis, keep the ongoing relationship even-keeled or show empathy for their situation, even if the second party is the most competent professional in their field, they will not be hired by the first party.

Individuals who have a more limited information gap about the professionals they hire are likely to treat psychology-based trust as important (and thus make retention of a professional anything but a purely rational decision). In the situation where the potential client truly does not understand the diagnosis and solution options for the matter at hand, trust building is almost exclusively a psychological process. Decisions are likely to be made based on soft factors as quiet confidence, the ability to listen and anticipate questions, and personal empathy. Most prospective clients have no real knowledge base of the subject at hand, Google searches notwithstanding. You should treat trust building as a psychological process. Of course you need to be technically skilled at evaluating the situation from a professional perspective. But the professional perspective will be meaningless unless the professional knows how to build trust with a potential client based on their psychological profile and needs.

Which brings us to the baseline trust mindset of the client or patient at the outset of an Insta-Trust meeting. Different individuals have different trust baselines. However, it is safe to say that the level of initial trust in another party at the beginning of a professional interaction under most circumstances is either nonexistent or moderate. From a psychological standpoint, you need to accept that at the beginning of an Insta-Trust meeting, the other person is likely going to be somewhat suspicious at best and perhaps outright hostile at worst. How do you overcome this level of baseline skepticism?

Through your demeanor, your questions and your empathy, you begin to build what I call knowledge-based trust. Knowledge-based trust is not trust based on your actual knowledge of the subject matter being discussed. Rather, knowledge-based trust is based on your ability to develop a strong interpersonal relationship with the other person based on your assessment of their personality and their personal and objective needs. In other words, you need to become knowledgeable, in a relatively short period of time, as to what makes the potential client tick and what really drives their decision making from a psychological and (to a more limited extent) rational perspective. You will know that you have begun to develop knowledge-based trust when the communication with the potential client becomes free-flowing and the shield that might have appeared at the beginning of the conversation from the potential client's standpoint has been lowered. You will know that you have thoroughly achieved knowledge-based trust when you have reached the stage in the conversation when your relationship appears to be collaborative (as opposed to skeptical or outright competitive). Once you achieve a collaborative stage, there is a high likelihood that the potential client will view their problem and your ability to help them as congruent and trust will be assumed. Once trust is assumed, you can move to the professional recommendation stage of the conversation and get yourself hired.

There is one more important point to discuss in this chapter. How important is trust in establishing a professional relationship? While there are negotiations between highly sophisticated parties who have world-class legal counsel and tightly drawn legal documents that provide for levels of penalties for trust breaking, outside of that limited world, trust is an essential element of a patient or client achieving a satisfactory outcome through information sharing. First, individuals who develop a trusting relationship with you are more likely to share information that enables you to develop a solution that can help the client. Second, information sharing helps you and the client develop solutions more quickly and, through the use of resources, in a far more efficient manner than if the parties deal with each other in a cautious manner, which typically equates to laborious information sharing. Third, trusting relationships allow the parties to avoid costly (i.e., in terms of wear and tear on a new relationship) monitoring arrangements in the future.

While trust is a far more desirable element in a nascent relationship, it is not essential in all situations, especially long-term business relationships. If the parties have the time to engage in a drawn-out information-sharing process and have a high degree of certainty that the cost of not performing under an agreement is excessively high, then each side will fulfill their end of what is being expected of them and the parties can move forward without a high level of trust. This is not a desirable way to engage in life, but you all have had to deal with bosses and other persons where you had little faith in their trustworthiness and you have been able to navigate (albeit with trepidation) to an acceptable conclusion.

"ONCE TRUST IS ASSUMED, YOU CAN MOVE TO THE PROFESSIONAL RECOMMENDATION STAGE OF THE CONVERSATION AND GET YOURSELF HIRED."

– Dr. Larry Jacobson

WHEELS OF INSTA-TRUST™:
Mutual Attraction

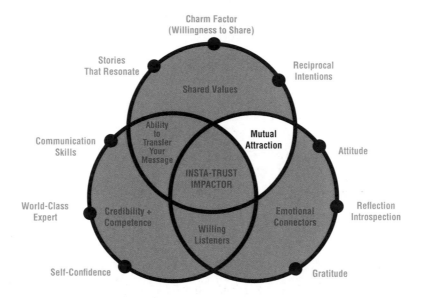

The Mutual Attraction concept in the WHEELS OF INSTA-TRUST™ applies to the ideas described in this chapter. When you develop Mutual Attraction, you do so by demonstrating the Emotional Connectors shown in the wheel, meaning showing gratitude, engaging in reflection with the other person and working with the other person with a positive and collaborative attitude. You also develop Mutual Attraction by demonstrating the Shared Values shown in the wheel, meaning the use of stories, the willingness to share and be compassionately candid, and engaging in reciprocal intentions in being open with each other. When you combine a Mutual Attraction mindset with a Shared Values mindset (as shown by the interlocking wheels), what do you get? You create a relationship that starts off on the right foot. You create a relationship that starts with an emotional bond that ripens into a personal and professional bond. It is like a firm handshake; the handshake is a metaphor for a personal relationship that should quickly develop into a mutually beneficial professional connection.

In summary, trust is not simply an expression to cause another person to feel better about a relationship. Once developed, trust allows the involved parties to more easily share information and a greater commitment to working together to reach a common goal. Conversely, the existence of little or no trust will likely result in the professional expending valuable time attempting to build a relationship with the prospective client, only to not get hired. Thus, trust is an extremely valuable resource that, in its own way, has a value equal to or greater than material resources. If the concept of time as having an economic value is true, then trust has its own economic value that can be measured through the value of your reputation. Your reputation is a function of the goodwill that exists in you personally and in your professional service organization. Treat every new Insta-Trust interaction as a way to build up your personal goodwill. You will find that you will naturally engage in a process that is designed to show your ability to help a prospective client and a sensitivity to what they are going through. Ability and sensitivity are a winning combination.

"TRUST IS AN EXTREMELY VALUABLE RESOURCE THAT, IN ITS OWN WAY, HAS A VALUE EQUAL TO OR GREATER THAN MATERIAL RESOURCES. IF THE CONCEPT OF TIME AS HAVING AN ECONOMIC VALUE IS TRUE, THEN TRUST HAS ITS OWN ECONOMIC VALUE THAT CAN BE MEASURED THROUGH THE VALUE OF YOUR REPUTATION."

Dr. Larry Jacobson

Ask Yourself

QUESTION ONE: Do I view trust building primarily from a psychological or a rational perspective?

QUESTION TWO: What techniques do I use at the very beginning of an Insta-Trust meeting to put the potential client at ease regarding the anxiety they are likely facing?

QUESTION THREE: How quickly am I assessing the other person's trust baseline and how do I adjust my interactions with them accordingly?

QUESTION FOUR: What techniques do I use to assess the areas (such as an information gap) that might be causing the potential client anxiety?

QUESTION FIVE: To what extent do I deliberately use sequencing in terms of how and when I bring up matters that, on the one hand, might be psychological in nature and, on the other hand, might be a technical issue that the potential client needs addressed?

QUESTION SIX: To what extent do I portray each potential solution to the potential client as bespoke and personalized to them?

QUESTION SEVEN: Do I treat my relationship-building skills as a valuable asset that needs to be nurtured and applied in every one of my professional interactions?

"FIRST SHOW THEM YOU CARE THROUGH YOUR EMOTIONAL CONNECTIONS, THEN SHOW THEM YOUR COMPETENCE."

Dr. Larry Jacobson

06

TRUST BUILDING 101: SHOW THEM HOW YOU CARE AS MUCH ABOUT THEM AS YOU DO ABOUT YOURSELF

"Everywhere I look I see your eyes."
– Rolling Stones

In the virtual world, you lack the face-to-face interactions that provide sensory perceptions (i.e., physical and auditory cues) that make it easier to size up the other person.

Research shows, and human experience confirms, that in most instances, the manner in which a message is delivered resonates more with recipients than the actual content of the message. Yet, it also appears that users of electronic communications tend to frame their messages from more of a rational perspective than one that recognizes the importance of emotion and psychology in influencing their audience. The savvy professional understands that they must be extra vigilant when using an electronic medium during an initial meeting with a prospective client than when first meeting face-to-face because such electronic meetings are almost always more challenging.

Experience shows that to build a trusting relationship on the phone, by email or by video conferencing, you must almost exclusively use personal persuasion techniques at the beginning of the conversation and not transition into a technical discussion too quickly. The goal is to motivate the potential client to accept the risk of moving forward by first building a relationship, then moving toward a collaborative decision-making approach and only then moving on to the technical aspects of the matter. Highly sophisticated clients might not want to spend an inordinate amount of time on relationship building, but even then a professional acts at his or her peril if they ignore the role that human relationships play in the retention process. So the beginning part of the initial conversation is showing that you care about them and their problem. Ask yourself the one thing you can do in the first 120 seconds of any conversation with Patricia that demonstrates you care about her as a person and the seriousness of her problem.

The absolute, 100 percent worst thing you can do at the beginning of a conversation with a new client is to explicitly ask them to "trust" you. Both research and experience shows individuals are almost always highly skeptical of others who brazenly assert their own trustworthiness. Put yourself in the position of a person who needs a knee replacement, like I did over eight years ago. The surgeon I used came highly recommended; in fact, he was so highly regarded that people came from all over the world to have him do their knee replacement, and he owned patents on certain types of implant prostheses. It was pretty clear this guy knew his stuff before we met. Yet how did this world-class surgeon win my trust over so quickly? We met (albeit in person, although the same conversation could have been done with video conferencing) and he showed me my X-ray that indicated there was no cartilage left and that I was walking with bone on bone. He explained that there was no nonsurgical option available to alleviate the pain. He asked me what type of lifestyle I wanted to lead after the knee replacement. We used that as a segue to a discussion about pain, the surgical process, recovery and what success looked like. The surgeon did that in a calm and reassuring manner that showed an incredibly high level of competence and confidence. The surgeon continuously asked if I had additional questions regarding the procedure and the rehabilitation process. Finally, at the end of the conversation, I asked him two additional questions. The first was an estimate of how many knee replacement surgeries he had done in the past 20 years. He laughed uproariously and said, "Larry, I have been asked a lot of questions by some pretty sharp people over the years, but never that one. I do surgeries on Monday and Thursday of each week, split between knee and hip replacements. That is all that I do, no other surgical procedures. I probably do surgeries an average of 40 to 42 weeks a year. You are a smart guy and you can do the math. However, that was a great question." If the surgeon gave me an actual number in a matter of seconds, I might not have viewed him nearly as trustworthy; how many surgeons can accurately or even semi-accurately determine in their heads in a flash how many surgeries they do in an average year? (Can you honestly state in a matter of seconds how many legal matters, tax returns, patient matters, etc., you work on in a year?) The second question I asked was what percentage of his surgeries did not turn out optimally for the patient. His response was, "I was about to get to that. No surgeon is perfect, and certain situations might not be correctable even if the surgical procedure is done flawlessly. However, and we do keep track of this, we estimate that around 94 percent of the knee replacement procedures we perform allow the patient to go back to a normal, pain-free existence, albeit with no running or physical sports." I ended the meeting by asking the surgeon if he could operate on me that afternoon. We had a good laugh and he thanked me for meeting with him. By the way, he was so booked that I needed to wait around four months before I underwent surgery.

In dissecting this conversation, a few things are notable. First, the surgeon never boasted about his background. He never had to, as his knowledge and bedside manner were so clearly evident by the manner in which he conducted the conversation. Second, because of his confidence level, he devoted at least 80 percent of the conversation to my comfort level with him and his explanation of his ability to help me get rid of my significant pain. Every word and every gesture he used was done with the sole objective of getting me to see, first from an emotional perspective, that he could help me through his surgical skills. Until we got toward the end of the conversation, there was only one technical aspect to the discussion—his showing me the X-ray at the very beginning of the conversation as conclusive evidence that surgery was the only option for my knee. After showing me the X-ray, the next 75 percent or so of the conversation had to do with me, the process, how he and his team would be with me every step of the way from presurgical preparation weeks before the surgery until I was discharged from physical therapy hopefully eight weeks after the surgery (he did such a great job on the surgery and I was a dutiful enough patient that I was done with physical therapy six weeks after surgery). Only toward the end of the conversation, after he had built rapport and clearly demonstrated a high level of competence, did we talk about the technical aspects of the surgery and recovery. Note the surgeon waited until we built personal trust before he explained his surgical competence and the recovery process. It was a lesson I use in my consulting practice every day.

My surgeon was an Insta-Trust Impactor. His approach can be defined as SHOWING THAT HE CARED MORE ABOUT ME THAN HIMSELF. He knew that patients came to see him to deal with a serious issue of importance to them. He also understood that most of the patients who came to him had at least some sense that he was an exceptional surgeon. Yet his ego did not require him to act in a boastful and dismissive manner. Rather, he was secure enough to understand that the person who needed persuasion was the patient. Your role in an initial interaction is not only to put Patricia at ease but to make her feel like you have a genuine personal interest in her successful outcome. Make the other person believe you are rowing the boat together.

Empathy is a word that is thrown around a lot, and the concept will be discussed in depth in the next chapter. Empathy is defined as the ability to understand the feelings of another and demonstrate that to the other person. Empathy demonstrates understanding; showing you care means your entire mindset and outlook are patient- or client-oriented. A professional can demonstrate empathy and still be egocentric in terms of attitude. For example, my surgeon could have clearly demonstrated that he understood my level of pain and why I was suffering but then could have abruptly transitioned into an early monologue as to his technique and his accomplishments. In doing so, he would have shown empathy for my pain while simultaneously demonstrating a total lack of recognition that I was a person whose concerns or fears needed to be addressed. While empathy is extremely important, you first need to show the prospective client or patient that you care about them and their situation on a human level.

"EMPATHY
DEMONSTRATES
UNDERSTANDING;
SHOWING YOU
CARE MEANS
YOUR ENTIRE
MINDSET AND
OUTLOOK ARE
PATIENT- OR
CLIENT-ORIENTED."

Dr. Larry Jacobson

Realistically, in most situations you have between the first one to five minutes to convince the other person that you deeply care about them and their problem. One effective way of doing that after the personal introduction is to ask them how they define their problem and what type of pain (which of course doesn't have to be physical) their problem is causing. After receiving the answer, keep asking open-ended questions designed to get them to open up about the pain being caused. Leave technical fact-finding questions until later. Focus on their perception of the problem, which might or might not be factually accurate. By asking a series of open-ended questions regarding their issue, you are showing concern.

Here are a few questions that can be asked of a Patricia in most professional interactions:

1. In a perfect world, what would it mean to you if I could help you with (put here the professional matter you are discussing and blend in the matter and how helping can alleviate their pain or accomplish their objective)? This question, unlike number 4 below, is designed to be open-ended so as to allow the other person to give a long, potentially emotion-based answer (rather than to discuss specific benefits that would be drawn out by question 4).

2. What problems that we are discussing keep you up at night? Are there any additional problems other than those that also keep you up at night?

3. Who will benefit, other than you, once we help you with your problem?

4. Name three things that you will achieve once we get your matter handled successfully.

5. Have you ever had a (put in your own professional activity here) matter similar to this one? If so, please tell me about your experience and how you felt once the matter was resolved.

Besides asking questions about them and their pain early in the conversation, it is vitally important that you constantly acknowledge that you understand them and their concerns. Indicate that you are sorry for what they are going through and that you are here to help them on a personal level as well as on a technical level.

There are many ways to show you care. My surgeon had a full-time nurse whose sole job was to answer questions about any part of the presurgical, surgical and postsurgical process at any time and to act as a conduit if I truly needed to speak with the surgeon. "Reggie" understood the anxieties patients have and would calmly answer any questions, logical or irrational, about the process. She acted as a perfect complement to the surgeon; having a process allowed the patient to ask questions beyond the first interaction with the surgeon and showed a depth of concern for the patient's physical and emotional well-being. You are not likely to get past first base with a prospective client unless you can clearly demonstrate you care about them as a person before you demonstrate you care about solving their problem. They can likely find any number of professionals who can actually solve their problem. Yet, whether they articulate it or not, what they are really looking for is a professional with whom they can work on both a human level and a technical/results level. You need to be as skillful, if not more skillful, in showing you care for them as a human as you are in actually solving their problem.

"YOU ARE NOT LIKELY TO GET PAST FIRST BASE WITH A PROSPECTIVE CLIENT UNLESS YOU CAN CLEARLY DEMONSTRATE YOU CARE ABOUT THEM AS A PERSON BEFORE YOU DEMONSTRATE YOU CARE ABOUT SOLVING THEIR PROBLEM."

– Dr. Larry Jacobson

However, in no way, shape or form should technical competence be ignored as part of the trust-building process. You can be the most caring person to a client or patient, but if you do not have the ability to help them with their problem, you are not only being deceitful, but you could cause the client or patient substantial physical or financial harm. Caring for a patient means sometimes admitting you are not the right professional for them. My surgeon would have been honest with me if I didn't need a knee replacement; he didn't need to operate on me for financial or ego purposes. Strive to be a professional who first thinks in terms of helping and caring for the client. It is OK to stretch your skill set and try new areas of expertise as long as you are guided by the lodestar that everything you do should be focused on how you can best serve the individual patient or client.

The following story is a personal example of how showing the other person you care about them in a volatile situation helps in getting a solution that is very specifically tailored to the person with whom you are interacting.

For a five-year period between 2000 and 2005, I was the Board Chair at a Jewish day school in Chicago. During the summer of 2004, we hired a new Head of School. Our philosophy as a Board was very simple; we hired the Head and the Head made all other employment decisions at the school. We did not micromanage the Head. The new Head spent most of her first year evaluating the administrators, teachers and other staff to see whether their skill set fit with her vision of the school moving forward.

The Head and I spoke several times a week as she asked me for advice on a wide variety of subjects and how to handle a number of sensitive matters. At one point, around two months before the end of the school year, she indicated that she was thinking of not renewing the contract of an administrator who worked at the school for well over a decade. I discussed the pros and cons with her over the span of a few weeks but reinforced that the decision either way had to be hers. The Head was struggling over the decision and I finally told her on a Monday that to be fair to the administrator, she needed to make a decision one way or another by that Friday. Sure enough, Friday afternoon came and went and no decision was made. Ironically, I developed a case of painful diverticulitis and had to go to the emergency room with my wife. While in the emergency room, the Head called me and said she was still unsure. Somehow, while in pain, I calmly told the Head that one of the critical aspects of being a leader was making timely decisions, even if they were tough ones. And she needed to make it right then. She decided not to offer the administrator a contract. So the first trust-building lesson of this exercise is to understand the role of time in deciding when to raise certain points during a conversation or series of conversations and then clearly demonstrate the importance of being firm about the need to make a decision about a course of action.

The following Monday, the Head and I met at the school; thanks to medication, my diverticulitis was treated over the weekend. We agreed on an approach where she would inform the administrator of the lack of a contract renewal. We knew the administrator would be disappointed (we were not sure if she would be surprised). Then, because I knew the administrator for a long period of time as someone who had worked with both of my children in the past and then in my role as Board Chair, I told the Head that it would be in everyone's best interest that I negotiate the severance agreement. As Board Chair, I had pretty broad authority to handle employment matters that did not involve litigation. We agreed on that approach.

As a trust-building exercise, this was a whole new ball game. I had trust with the administrator in her role at the school, but she had no idea if I was going to be trustworthy in this new setting. Sure enough, she hired counsel and I agreed to meet with the administrator privately (not as an attorney) but as Board Chair to come to an appropriate settlement.

So this was a situation where trust existed, it was broken (through no fault of my own) and it needed to be rebuilt. Even in long-term relationships, sometimes trust ebbs and flows and then gets re-established. In this case, even though I was not viewed as the trust breaker (she knew I had zero role in her termination), I needed to build trust with her as if it was a new professional relationship. So we began the process.

I let her vent. She asked me for an honest assessment of her strengths and weaknesses. Once that question was asked, I saw that trust building was going to occur through a coaching approach that took into account emotion. I was asked if we could disregard our prior relationship and start from scratch in terms of looking at her career. She agreed.

I pointed out that she had excellent interpersonal skills and was quite good at the nonacademic aspects of her position. Then I stated from my perspective she needed to beef up the academic part of her repertoire. I told her if she did that, her job prospects would be enhanced. I ended the meeting stating she should take my thoughts under advisement and that our goal was to build her post-employment career together. In other words, I was being fully other-centered. We agreed to meet next week.

I told the Head after the meeting with the administrator what I did and how I was going to handle the matter. When I met with the administrator the following week, she appreciated my candor and concern for her beyond her employment at the school. She was explicit in stating her trust in me in this troubling setting (and not in the Head). I told her I was appreciative of her comments. Then I showed her trust in me by not just offering a generous financial severance, but also proposing to pay 100 percent of her tuition and books to obtain a master's degree. The master's would make her far more employable for another academic position. Between the severance and the offer to pay for a master's, I came up with an other-centered solution that met her very specific situation. After speaking with her attorney, we came to an agreement. During the last six weeks of her employment, she did not speak to the Head and all communications with the Head were through me, because she built fast trust with me in a new setting and I looked out for what I truly thought was her best interest.

The lesson I learned is that you might think you have trust with someone you know, but if the environment changes, you need to build fast initial trust as if you are starting a new professional relationship.

WHEELS OF INSTA-TRUST™:
Emotional Connectors

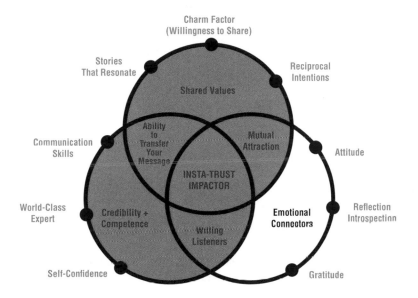

The Emotional Connector concept in the WHEELS OF INSTA-TRUST™ applies to the ideas described in this chapter. When you develop an Emotional Connection, you do so by demonstrating the Emotional Connectors on the wheel, meaning showing gratitude, engaging in reflection with the other person and working with the other person with a positive and collaborative attitude. Emotional Connection is the most powerful connection you can develop. You can develop a relationship that is built on mutual economic interests or other noneconomic interests such as maintaining power over others. Solely economic or power-based relationships can disintegrate quickly if the economic circumstances change or the need for the power alliance becomes tenuous or nonexistent. But if you have a deep Emotional Connection with a client or patient, your relationship can weather changes in economic circumstances or the external environment. But you need to continuously demonstrate the key Emotional Connector behaviors of having a positive and egoless attitude, displaying gratitude for the relationship and engaging in reflection as to how the relationship can be taken to the next level. An Emotionally Connected relationship between two parties is a professional relationship that can reap huge rewards for both sides.

At the end of this chapter and at the end of some of the later chapters, I am going to discuss how the main chapter topic applies to each of the 11 archetypes described in Chapter Two. The techniques to be used in deploying the main chapter topic varies based on the personality traits demonstrated by the potential patient/client. One size does not fit all in terms of how you build the different components of trust.

For each of the archetypes discussed in this chapter and the later chapters, please ask yourself the following two questions:

1. Who do you know that fits this archetype?

2. What are three things you could do to build Insta-Trust with this archetype?

Here are the well-defined archetypes:

THE CLOSE-TO-THE-VEST. Our initial default setting in starting a virtual interaction with a potential patient or client should be treating them as having an unknown personality type. When you start out with an open mind, you have a blank canvas to use in assessing the person before you. With the truly unknown person (meaning it is not immediately evident at the beginning of the interaction what their real interests are), the professional should ask a variety of questions to assess their anxiety level, how inquisitive they are about the matter being discussed, their level of risk tolerance and how open they are to having a candid conversation. Once you get a preliminary sense of how the potential client measures on these factors, you can assess which other personality archetype you need to tailor your approach to in order to successfully show them you care.

THE TOUGH NUT. The tough nut is someone who very early on in your interaction demonstrates a high level of skepticism. Basically, they are in a show-me mood. Your inclination is that by showing them you care, you let them dictate the tone and direction of the conversation. You might think the best approach is to go directly to the technical aspect of the problem and how you can solve it. That approach would be wrong. Your goal should be to maintain a level of quiet confidence and competence. If anything, you should ask more questions about their anxiety and risk level as they relate to the matter at hand. You should really dwell on their pain point and pain tolerance. You gain the confidence of the tough nut in terms of showing you care by taking as much time as necessary to demonstrate you care about them personally and their problem. Then move toward telling them how you can solve their problem. In most instances, you crack the tough nut through patience.

THE KNOW-IT-ALL. Most of the time, the know-it-all doesn't actually know it all. Showing a know-it-all you care is very tricky because you will have to dissuade them of a deeply held belief that they know quite a bit about the subject matter being discussed. Again, the inclination is to basically show the other person you know your stuff very early on in the conversation. My recommendation is not to do that. Some know-it-alls really do think they are highly knowledgeable on the subject matter, but many are insecure and use the know-it-all personality as a defense mechanism. The more you can ask penetrating questions, much like with the tough nut, the more you can demonstrate a blend of a caring personality and competence in a calm and non-egotistical manner. The know-it-all will know that you care when you show that you are willing to work with them, even when their assumptions are found lacking, and that you are more concerned about their problem than proving them wrong.

THE NOVICE. This is a person who truly knows nothing about the matter being discussed. You can generally sense if someone is a novice very early in the conversation. Once their novice status becomes evident, then your approach in showing them you care should be to ask a lot of questions about how the matter being discussed impacts them personally. The more pertinent personal questions you ask (and the questions have to be as pertinent as they are personal), the more you demonstrate you care about them. Once that caring relationship is established, it becomes easy to move to the technical part of the discussion, but your job is not over. The novice is likely to ask a lot of technical questions that show a lack of understanding. You need to answer those questions with additional patience.

THE TIRE KICKER. The tire kicker might be the most frustrating personality type to deal with. Your efforts are to draw them out to discover their concerns, fears and problem. Yet when you feel you are done with the relationship-building part of the conversation and try to get them to focus on the technical aspects of the problem, they appear distant or uninterested. Your job is to try to determine if they are truly indecisive as to whether you are the right person for the matter at hand. If their indecisiveness appears genuine, you should show them that you care by acknowledging their hedging approach and ask them directly what other questions you can answer in order to make them more comfortable. But if they continue to be disinterested, then you need to decide whether the other person is someone who would be the right type of client or patient for you. True tire kickers are rarely appreciative of the professionals they work with.

THE INDECISIVE. This person has a tough time making up their mind. They know they have a problem and know they need to have it solved. They just don't know whether the issue is urgent or you are the one to help them. How you show an indecisive person that you care about them is to spend a lot of time explaining your experience in helping similar individuals with similar problems. Prove you have the ability to help them very specifically and show them evidence to that point. Then tell them you really think you can help them. In fact, the best thing you can do to show an indecisive person that you care about them is, at the appropriate stage of the conversation, to acknowledge their ambivalence and quietly state you are the person who can help them and want their representation.

THE LONG-TIMER. The long-timer might be the easiest archetype to show that you care about them as a person. If you discern the person you are meeting with is a long-timer, you should spend a disproportionate amount of time working on relationship building. Only after you feel you have established a strong personal rapport with the other person, then you can transition into problem solving. It is possible that the problem-solving conversation might take place in a second meeting; many long-timers want to spend an initial meeting building a personal relationship. A true long-timer is likely looking for a long-term personal relationship that morphs into a professional relationship. Think of giving them examples of clients or patients that have been working with you for 10 or 20 years or longer. Offer to get them in touch with your long-term clients or patients with whom you have a very strong personal bond. Also, with the long-timer, impress on them that you are not only interested in solving the problem they brought to you, but that you care about them more holistically. Make the long-timer *feel* that you will go the extra mile in helping them as a person, not just as a problem to be solved.

THE SCHOOMZER. Ah, the person who likes to talk. And talk. Even the most patient professional does not have all the time in the world to listen to a schmoozer whose main goal appears to be either to hear themselves talk or to engage in lengthy inanities. The best way to show a schmoozer you care is to address their purpose head on. Of course, you want to hear out the relevant aspects of their problem and anxiety. You want to glean the relevant facts that can help you help them. But once the conversation goes off the rails into irrelevant areas, the best way you can show them you care is by simply telling them that you want to help them, but it is not fair to them to waste time. Rather, ask them if they were in your shoes, would they want to spend needless time on impertinent discussions rather than time better used in helping you? Most of the time that helps focus the schmoozer. If not, ask yourself if it is a relationship worth having.

THE KNOWLEDGEABLE. The knowledgeable prospective client or patient appears to be an easy one to work with. But beware. They might be knowledgeable but have a secondary archetype personality, such as a long-timer or a tough nut. So even though they have a high knowledge base, you might have to work with them in a manner where the discussion might still need to be rather lengthy. When I say lengthy, I do not mean to minimize the early part of the conversation that focuses on relationship building and demonstrating a collaborative approach. In fact, the most important thing you can do with a knowledgeable client is impress on them that you really view the relationship as a partnership and that you deeply respect their knowledge base. You also can acknowledge the ancillary organizational, political and other pressures that might be impacting them and their problem. Showing the knowledgeable you care is the absolute best way to create a smooth segue into a meaningful technical discussion. So don't give short shrift to the relationship building even if the other person is knowledgeable.

THE QUICK DRAW. The quick draw likes to make decisions quickly. They view themselves as decisive. Frequently, they like to dispense with social niceties and "get down to business." You should acknowledge that they want to get down to business quickly and make a quick decision as to whether to hire you. But to show that you care, indicate that your process is not designed to unnecessarily drag out the process but to ask questions that, based on your professional experience, are designed to uncover the facts of the situation and their actual and latent concerns. Inform them you won't ask anything impertinent or spend more time than is necessary to help reach the technical stage of the conversation. And then do exactly that. If you can show that you respect their time (and for the quick draw, time is what they are most concerned about) by using time very efficiently to draw out facts and concerns to come up with optimal solutions, you will be showing the quick draw you are in control and sensitive to what they care about most.

THE EGOMANIAC. Ah, the egomaniac. How do you prove to someone that you care about them and their problem when they care (almost) exclusively about themselves? Very, very carefully. With the egomaniac, you need to carefully balance their perceived need for recognition and control with your need to control the relationship with quiet confidence and competence. If you let the egomaniac completely control the conversation, you will lose the ability to help them. As important, you will probably lose their respect, so they will likely view you as a lackey who is not able to help them. The goal with the egomaniac is to let them get things off their chest at the get-go and then very firmly and quietly let them know you are there to help them, but only if the two of you can work together, without ego or histrionics and as true collaborators. Egomaniacs need to be gently put in their place through demonstration of confidence and competence. Most egomaniacs will respect you if you show firmness in your dealings. They will never let go of their high opinion of themselves; your job is to maintain your professional approach and desire to help them with their problem. With the egotist, you need to convince them you care by literally telling them your role is to make them look good in the eyes of others. After all of this, if their ego is still in the way, drop them like a hot potato. The extreme egomaniac is not only self-centered but will loudly blame you for all of their issues, however undeserved that might be.

Ask Yourself

QUESTION ONE: Do I have a naturally caring personality when it comes to helping others? If not, how do I intend to develop one?

QUESTION TWO: How do I display quiet confidence with new clients and patients?

QUESTION THREE: Do I have a 3-to-5-minute process to show the other person I care deeply about them and their problem?

QUESTION FOUR: How do I display quiet confidence with new clients and patients or in a negotation setting?

QUESTION FIVE: Do I put relationship building before problem solving when I meet a new client or patient?

QUESTION SIX: What is my ability to assess their personality archetype?

QUESTION SEVEN: Have I developed the skill set to blend the types of questions I need in an initial encounter: caring questions, technical questions and solution-oriented questions?

"THE HEAD MUST LEAD THE HEART TO THE RELATIONSHIP."

Dr. Larry Jacobson

07

TRUST BUILDING 102: IT'S ABOUT EMPATHY, STUPID.

"Data informs but the heart decides."
– Dr. Larry Jacobson

Empathy is an incredibly complicated emotion. Frequently, empathy is misunderstood. Even more frequently, empathy is grossly misused by professionals in initial conversations.

"EMPATHY POORLY DISPLAYED MAY BE MORE DAMAGING TO A PROFESSIONAL RELATIONSHIP THAN ANY OTHER POTENTIAL FAUX PAS."

– Dr. Larry Jacobson

Your skill at determining the points of vital importance to your potential client or patient is your gathering the "data" that will help you assess how to develop a relationship with the other person. Developing that relationship first involves the interpersonal "soft" data assessment and then developing strategies that are targeted to the heart of the potential client. Empathy involves first understanding their problem and then showing them you are emotionally and professionally invested in helping them solve their problem. The head must lead the heart to the relationship.

The common definition of empathy is the ability to understand the feelings of another. In theory, someone who is excellent at showing empathy also has the ability to "read the mind" of the other person in order to figure out not only their feelings but how deep and significant those feelings might be. You may remember the comment of former President Clinton during the 1992 presidential election campaign when he told someone, "I feel your pain."

What is the difference between mind reading and the professional assessment of a potential client's or patient's mindset? If someone clearly demonstrates by word, tone and body language that a problem is physically or mentally bothering them, then it is easy to feel their pain and acknowledge it quickly and with great effect. However, if the person is either inarticulate or is unwilling at the outset to share in a profound manner the level of personal or physical discomfort they are currently facing, how do you "feel their pain"?

"SHOW EMPATHY THROUGH YOUR ACTIONS AND WORDS, BUT NOT THROUGH USING THE TIRED CLICHÉ OF TELLING THEM YOU FEEL THEIR PAIN."

– Dr. Larry Jacobson

If you are totally honest with yourself, you should acknowledge that mind reading is not a skill you were taught in medical school, dental school, law school, business school, etc. The same is true if you are a deal maker who is trying to "read" the mind of the other party to see what problem they are trying to solve in the negotiation. Moreover, mind reading is not a skill that improves with experience in the real world. When showing empathy in an initial client contact, you should eliminate the notion that somehow you can really feel the pain of the other person.

In building Insta-Trust, you should demonstrate empathy by asking a lot of questions about their problem. Ask questions that are relationship based. Ask them about themselves, their problem and how their problem is impacting their personal and professional lives. Ask them about what solving the problem will do in terms of improving their personal or professional life. Ask that particular question with tremendous feeling. Take notes and refer back to them when you ask follow-up questions. The more you can get them to think that you are genuinely concerned about the impact a successful outcome will have on them, the further you are on the road to demonstrating true empathy.

In meetings by phone or video conferencing, the other person either cannot see you, or if they can, they are not getting the full display of visual cues to see that you are empathetic. In those settings, it is even more vital to use tone of voice in your questioning and dialogue to show you are genuinely concerned about them and their problem. In fact, in these settings, showing empathy does NOT involve showing them you feel their pain. Rather, what you are trying to do is diagnose their pain and how it impacts them. By professionally using questions to diagnose their pain, you are showing far more empathy than by calling yourself out as empathetic.

In my experience, professionals who attempt to use the Clintonian feel-their-pain approach frequently come off as phony. Bill Clinton could generally get away with this approach because of his incredible interpersonal skills. But even Clinton's approach wore thin after a while because it raised credibility issues. Once again, how could he *really* feel a person's pain? Clinton had a different intellectual perspective, a different worldview, a different economic perspective from the ordinary citizens with whom he interacted.

But there is a huge difference between "feeling" their pain and acknowledging their discomfort and the level of discomfort. Your goal is to understand their discomfort. Through questioning and reinforcement, show them that you understand (1) them as an individual, (2) their problem, (3) the seriousness of the problem and (4) the need to develop a personalized solution to deal with their problem.

Earlier I said that telling someone they can "trust you" frequently creates the opposite effect; they are less likely to trust someone who self-identifies as trustworthy. Likewise, if a professional tells someone that they are feeling their pain (as opposed to saying, based on a strong line of questioning and display of genuine emotion, that they understand their situation), they frequently come off as lacking in credibility. Understanding, not misguided feelings, builds empathy.

Understanding the approach toward showing empathy does not mean you should be devoid of showing an appropriate level of emotion involving the client and their problem. To the contrary, showing professional emotion involves an approach that cannot and should not come off as robotic. Within the bounds of maintaining the appropriate boundaries, you should show through voice tone and eye contact (during face-to-face or video conferencing meetings) a strong level of empathy. You can best show empathy, beyond the sensitive questioning approach, through nonverbal communication. Tone and, where appropriate, eye contact should be your main non-verbal tools to convey professional emotion and let them know that you DEEPLY understand their situation and will work with them to come up with the solution that works for them.

Another tool in showing empathy is the appropriate use of humor at the right time. The use of humor, not to demean the client or their problem, but as a skillful way to defuse a potentially tense situation, can prevent a scenario from becoming overly dramatic. Most of the time when you are being asked to work on an issue, it is a very serious matter for the client. For example, if you are an attorney and someone is thinking of hiring you to handle a high-stakes (to the client) litigation or corporate matter, their level of concern, angst and need for a great result may be at an absolute fever pitch. If you are a surgeon, their level of concern about their diagnosis, the treatment plan (including possible surgery) and chances of full recovery is at an absolute fever pitch. If you are a CPA and the potential client is being audited by the IRS, everything about the issue (especially the fear of the IRS) is incredibly concerning. Straight humor might not be appropriate in these settings.

Your questions and tone need to match the seriousness of the matter. Nevertheless, the surgical (pun intended), subtle use of humor, can help show that you are understanding their problem. If you are being interviewed to be hired to sue someone on a personal injury matter, you can tell the client that, "I have gone up against that insurance company many times and I own those bastards. I won (then list the dollar recoveries you have made against that insurance company) and I don't intend to lose your case." If you are a surgeon, list a few great results of prior patients (offer to have the prospective patient contact them if you have their consent) and state matter-of-factly (if true), "I don't waste my time golfing or messing around on frivolous interests. If we work together, you are getting the best damn surgeon in this city." If you are a CPA, you simply state, "I hate the IRS as much as you do. I am so motivated to kick their ass that I am frothing at the mouth to start this very minute to help you." By using subtle humor in demonstrating your exceptionally strong commitment to the client's or patient's situation, you develop an emotional connection with them—an emotional connection that should resonate with a potential client and get them fired up to hire you.

The final element of showing empathy is, as mentioned in the prior paragraph, the effective use of referrals. If humanly possible, you should have a list of prior clients or patients for whom you not only did a great job, but who are evangelists for you—people who will honestly and enthusiastically sing your praises from a technical standpoint and from the standpoint of emotional connection and how you dealt with them with respect, understanding and as a collaborator. By offering up a list of referrals at the appropriate time during the initial conversation, you are demonstrating quiet confidence. You are building trust by showing the potential client your prior successes and that you relate to your clients on a human level. Prior great success, plus showing understanding of the person and their issue through deep questions, plus great referrals, equals powerful empathy.

The following story is a personal example showing that the patient use of empathy can achieve a satisfactory result in a high-stakes situation.

After a major acquisition, my corporate client decided to terminate the chief executive of the company they acquired. The chief executive was not in favor of the acquisition and his personality did not mesh with the acquiring company. As is the case in many large company acquisitions, the target company executives had severance agreements that specified substantial cash-out payments for salary, lost pension, bonuses and fringe benefits. The chief executive had this type of severance agreement.

The chief executive was emotional about the acquisition and his termination. In business, he was a cool and calculated executive and was quite logical about corporate strategy. But in this case, he was livid and asked his counsel to come up with legal arguments to squeeze more money out of our client corporation.

The employment contract was pretty straightforward and well drafted. The amount my client claimed was owed to the chief executive was the amount that any reasonable attorney or judge would likely state was due. My client had zero desire to shortchange the chief executive out of his rightful severance. But any excellent attorney can find some arguments to buttress a case that looks bulletproof. The chief executive asked his attorney to scorch the earth to find any loophole possible and threaten litigation if necessary. Obviously, it was not my client's preferred position to litigate and start out on the wrong foot with some of the target company's employees, but there was a limit as to how much they would pay for what they viewed as "blackmail."

So the client asked me to try to settle the matter out of court. Along with one of my partners, I contacted the chief executive's counsel and offered to meet an independent mediator to see if we could settle the matter out of court. Opposing counsel agreed to meet with us and the mediator. Our instructions were simple; we were given a dollar amount above the amount we felt was due under the contract and told we could settle for any amount at or below that dollar amount. Our client did not want the negative publicity of a lawsuit or the possibility of senior executives having to testify at a trial.

A key strategic move I made was to not put a limit on the length of the mediation. I felt that if we created a self-imposed time limit on the mediation, little would be accomplished and a lawsuit would follow. Sure enough, during the first day of the mediation, the chief executive vented (and to be fair, his attorney did the right thing to let him vent). On day two, the chief executive vented. The mediator, an experienced and wise attorney, asked a few questions of the chief executive about his feelings (and no questions about contract interpretation) during day one and two, but like us, allowed the chief executive to vent. At the beginning of day three, the mediator asked counsel on both sides to present him with their technical arguments, which we did in a matter of around a half hour. Then the mediator offered to meet with us to give his assessment of the case; mediators don't often offer assessments of a case because their job is to move the parties to do that on their own, but in situations where emotions run high, they sometimes will give their view of the strength of each side's legal position. That gave me the opening I needed.

In order to build trust with the chief executive and his counsel, I needed to let the chief executive do his venting. This was personal; he was going to get a mid-seven-figure severance in any event. He needed to be heard. Those two days of venting and doing little to rebut the sometimes wild assertions of the chief executive built trust. Sometimes you build trust with what you don't say more than by what you do say. So I asked the mediator to leave the room so I could speak with the chief executive and his attorney. Once the mediator left the room, I made a very brief presentation. I stated that I was sorry that the chief executive was in the predicament he was in. I said he was a highly gifted professional and he had a bright future in his industry. I added that if I was in his position, I would have been pissed off that my client never gave me a chance to stay with the company. I then took a piece of paper from my legal pad and tore it in half. After I tore the paper, I said that once the paper is torn, it cannot be put back in the original condition. I said that was a metaphor for a divorce, be it a marital divorce or the equivalent employment arrangement. The divorce will cause angst and likely will do so for an extended period. But you need to move on after the decision until the divorce is final. I told the executive that the decision to divorce employment was final and we were doing the equivalent of a divorce settlement agreement. In this case, we had the equivalent of a prenuptial agreement and it was not in his best interest to challenge it because if the dispute became public, it could adversely impact his future employment prospects. Big corporations do not like hiring individuals who sue their prior employers.

At that point, I told him we would be willing to pay him for the pain and suffering above the amount due under his severance agreement. He took a private meeting with his counsel and then came back to ask for the number. We gave them a number and within 15 minutes we agreed on a number satisfactory to both sides. The chief executive went on to a highly successful business career due to his high skill level. Before, during and after our mediation I had a high opinion of the chief executive and wanted him to engage in a separation that valued him yet protected our client's position.

The lesson of this trust-building exercise is you need to know when to hold them (meaning let the other person speak even if it doesn't appear to push the situation forward in a linear manner) and when to fold them (meaning that you need to have the awareness as to when to move on from the conversation and build trust by words and not just listening). In this case, the process worked. Frankly, the most gratifying aspect of the process was not the result for our client, which was perfectly acceptable. I was far more pleased that the chief executive bounced back from this setback and has had a great career. My empathy in this situation was genuine, and I was able to represent my client's interests successfully and gain a good result for the other side because of the fact that I realized any of us could be jilted in a professional setting.

"SOMETIMES YOU BUILD TRUST WITH WHAT YOU DON'T SAY MORE THAN WITH WHAT YOU DO SAY."

– Dr. Larry Jacobson

WHEELS OF INSTA-TRUST™:
Ability to Transfer Your Message

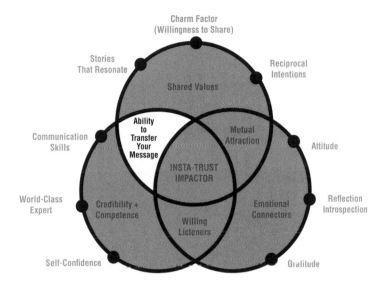

The Ability to Transfer your Message concept applies to the ideas described in this chapter. When you can successfully transfer your message, you do so by demonstrating the concepts of Shared Values and Credibility and Competence that are shown in the interlocking portion of the Wheel. As a world-class expert who demonstrates quiet self-confidence, your technical abilities are evident without the need for excessive bragging. You express those skills through communication that blends the technical and the emotional. You show your emotional communication skills through effective nonverbal communication, the use of stories and demonstrating you understand the other person, both from a human perspective and from the standpoint of a problem solver. The novice professional treats communication as simply a means to show the other person how you want to get from Point A to Point B. The Insta-Trust Impactor who is highly competent views communication as an auditory and visual process where the goal is not just to get the other person to hire them (or in the case of a negotiation, reach an excellent solution), but to develop a sense of Shared Values. BECAUSE SHARED VALUES AND HIGH COMPETENCE = A PROFESSIONAL RELATIONSHIP BUILT ON TRUST AND A GOAL THAT THE OTHER PERSON KNOWS YOU WILL KNOCK DOWN WALLS TO ACHIEVE.

Now on to the archetypes:

THE CLOSE-TO-THE-VEST. After asking a couple of preliminary questions about the nature of the problem (if not already known by virtue of a pre-meeting referral or a pre-meeting communication from the potential client), do a deep dive into relationship building. Ask them about how the problem is impacting them on a personal (or business) level. Ask them what a successful outcome would be. Ask them about how a successful outcome would impact them and their family (or business if appropriate). Once you develop a personal relationship, then get into how you will help them. Yes, talk about the technical aspects, using lay language, but continue to show quiet confidence in your abilities. If they open up, then be a little more forceful about your ability to help them. If not, think about the use of referrals to boost your profile with the prospective client.

THE TOUGH NUT. The tough nut is a skeptic. As such, it can be very difficult to get a tough nut to show empathy or respond positively to empathy. If you think you are dealing with a tough nut, do not go overboard in terms of displaying emotion or empathy. Rather, bore into the real pain point of the problem, asking lots of questions regarding the problem and the impact of the problem on them (or their business). By asking them questions of this sort, you are likely to display as much empathy as the tough nut is willing to accept. A tough nut might never allow you to develop a deep personal relationship. As such, maximum empathy for a tough nut is your ability to matter-of-factly demonstrate you understand them and their issue and lay out the proposed solution that works best for them. Also, the targeted use of referral contacts can reduce their skepticism. Use other tough nuts as referrals to potential tough nut clients.

THE KNOW-IT-ALL. In terms of demonstrating empathy to the know-it-all, patience is the key to building a relationship. They think they know it all. In fact, they might not know about the depth of the problem or the solution, but they might not even have adequate self-awareness about themselves. You will have to systematically listen to their alleged knowledge of the depth of the problem or the solution. Once you have given them a chance to spout off, then you can ask preliminary questions, showing you care about them as a person. Then you morph into a list of questions regarding the problem, how it impacts them and how a solution would positively help them. In terms of the know-it-all, you need to ask questions to show quiet competence. It is essential that you keep control of the conversation, both in terms of direction and the matters to be discussed. Know-it-alls can tend to dominate the conversation, and if you allow that to happen, you will find it difficult to demonstrate true empathy and build real trust.

THE NOVICE. When you are dealing with a person who lacks understanding of the problem at hand (other than the fact that they know they have a problem), empathy starts from the very beginning. You start by stating your understanding of the problem and then move very quickly into asking questions on a very personal level—about their background, how they discovered the problem, how it impacts them and how your help will impact their life. Once you build rapport, then you use tone and (if possible) eye contact to demonstrate personal empathy. Then you build professional empathy by confidently explaining to them how you are going to solve their problem and how it will help them achieve their personal or professional objectives. The goal in terms of building an empathetic relationship with a novice is to acknowledge their lack of knowledge and insecurity in a manner that shows them you will take as much time as is reasonably necessary to assuage their concerns.

THE TIRE KICKER. Tire kickers are incredibly frustrating to deal with. You don't know whether they are seriously interested in hiring you or whether they get their kicks from wasting the time of multiple professionals. Since you don't know at the beginning of the conversation whether the tire kicker is interested in working with you, after asking a couple of questions about the problem, move quickly into the personal relationship-building questions. If after asking a half dozen questions or so, you sense they are not taking you with the appropriate level of seriousness, you may as well go for broke and say that you would like to represent them, but they are going to show the appropriate respect for you and your time. They must be willing to help you help them. By putting the empathy issue on those terms, you are quite clear that you want to help them, but respect for you and your time is essential. The tire kicker needs to understand that empathy and trust are a two-way street and they need to demonstrate the desire to carry their share of the relationship. If you don't discern a desire on their part to invest in the relationship, move on.

THE INDECISIVE. Empathy for the indecisive starts with a meaningful discussion of the potential client's issue and pain point. But since the indecisive starts out ambivalent about you personally and your technical skills, you need to spend a fair amount of time with them creating empathy through building a personal relationship. For the indecisive, gaining their heart first is more important than accessing their brain. Once you gain their heart through empathy-building questions regarding them, demonstrate your technical skills through quiet confidence and the offer to speak with your satisfied clients. The goal in successfully gaining the empathy of an indecisive client is to nudge them into making a decision to hire you by demonstrating your deep desire to represent them.

THE LONG-TIMER. When dealing with a deliberative person, look at the situation as an opportunity. They are not only looking at someone who can help them solve their problem, but someone they might want a long-term professional relationship with. To them, the relationship is as important as the technical capabilities of the individual (think of your long-term relationships with your internist, CPA, dentist, attorney, etc.). Thus, for the person who comes across early on as a potential long-timer, once you have the brief initial discussion about their problem, build empathy by spending as much time as possible learning about them as an individual. Show you have a deep interest in them, their problem and their pain. Don't insult them by saying you feel their pain. Rather, tell them that you are taking a personal interest in them and solving their problem. After relationship building, demonstrate quiet confidence and competence. Then, if appropriate, state you would love to work with them on their issues for years to come and engage in a more aggressive mode of asking them to work with you. That's how you can build empathy with some long-timers.

THE SCHMOOZER. On the surface, building empathy with a schmoozer would appear to be an easy task. Not necessarily. With the schmoozer, you need to first take control of the conversation and not let them speak incessantly and indefinitely. Let them get their concerns out in the open, but control the situation. Ask targeted questions about them and their issues, but keep the questions to a minimum. Then, show quiet confidence by continuing to control the conversation. Do not allow diversions or distractions. Tell them how you have helped others with similar problems. Allow them to ask questions and answer them with short and targeted responses. Build empathy by responding directly to their concerns and your capabilities, but don't let the conversation drag. Then ask them if they have any further questions before they hire you. In other words, assume the close.

THE KNOWLEDGEABLE. When dealing with a person who is knowledgeable about the matter at hand, there is a tendency to avoid the empathy part of the conversation. Don't. Even the most knowledgeable client needs you to demonstrate empathy. Empathy for them as a person. Empathy for the conundrum they are facing. Empathy for the gravity of the matter to them. In other words, for the knowledgeable, showing empathy first is the key to building a professional relationship. If you can demonstrate empathy first, then the discussion regarding the technical aspects of the matter will go much more smoothly. By demonstrating personal empathy at the outset of the conversation and then demonstrating a high technical skill level, the knowledgeable will be ready to hire you. They can find plenty of highly skilled professionals. For the knowledgeable, finding a professional who also makes a concerted effort to relate to them personally is rare and places you in the driver seat.

THE QUICK DRAW. Like the knowledgeable, the assumption is to believe that the quick draw wants to get down to business and discard the interpersonal aspect of the professional relationship. While you might not engage in lengthy conversation in terms of asking them about how the matter impacts them personally (or professionally), do not ignore empathy building with the quick draw. Even if they are more intellectual or rational than emotional in their decision making, ignoring their emotional concerns is a big mistake. Very early on in the conversation, acknowledge that they are quick decision makers, but you want to take a little time to understand the depth of their concerns and how the problem impacts them. By doing that, you demonstrate both the need to show empathy about them as an individual and respect for their decision-making process. Keep the conversation on point and show confidence in your abilities. This is critical with a quick draw. By confidence, I mean quiet confidence to start out and then move to more demonstrable confidence (including the use of prior successes and referrals) to get them to make a quick decision to hire you. For the quick draw, social proof is a strong way to build empathy.

THE EGOMANIAC. It is very challenging to build an empathetic relationship with an egomaniac. They care about themselves and may view your efforts to connect with them as a diversion. Frankly, you might not even attempt to build traditional empathy with an egomaniac. Getting to the point with the egomaniac is probably the best approach. Ask them if they want to discuss the personal aspects of the issue, and if they say no, don't press the point. If they say yes, ask them questions about how fixing the problem will make them look better to others. Then move to the professional aspects of the conversation, but show quiet confidence about the relationship by subtly dominating the conversation. Show your expert status by asking piercing questions and demonstrating a high level of competence. Show that you are the boss of your domain and you have a long track record of success. In other words, demonstrate that you have worked with other egomaniacs before (although of course don't label it as such) in a highly successful manner and the two of you can find a way to work together as well. This might not demonstrate empathy in the traditional sense, but in the mind of the egomaniac, showing that you will stand up to him or her when necessary in order to help them achieve their goal is a unique type of empathy, as you are truly understanding them and how to help them.

Ask Yourself

QUESTION ONE. Do I understand my inability to truly read the minds of the Patricias who might want me to work with them?

QUESTION TWO. Do I understand the role of asking penetrating questions and how asking the right penetrating questions builds quick empathy?

QUESTION THREE. How does building empathy move a professional relationship forward?

QUESTION FOUR. Can a professional relationship exist without some level of empathy on the part of the professional and, if so, under what circumstances?

QUESTION FIVE. Do I truly have the ability to identify when the potential client senses my empathy for them?

QUESTION SIX. Do I know how and when it might be appropriate to start developing empathy through the initial attempt of a technical discussion of the matter rather than the initial attempt of building a personal relationship?

QUESTION SEVEN. Do I consider the role of humor in building empathy during challenging conversations or when I need to demonstrate in a non-bragging manner my ability to help them?

"PRIOR GREAT
SUCCESS, PLUS
SHOWING
UNDERSTANDING
OF THE PERSON
AND THEIR
ISSUE THROUGH
DEEP QUESTIONS,
PLUS GREAT
REFERRALS, EQUALS
POWERFUL EMPATHY."

Dr. Larry Jacobson

TRUST BUILDING 103:
THE SECRET TO ACTIVE LISTENING
THAT BUILDS TRUST

"Time may change me, but I can't trace time."
– David Bowie

Trust building is a process where time is an essential element. Even if you are with a potential client or patient for 10 or 15 minutes, every second and every word counts. The purpose of the interaction with the potential client or patient is to hopefully hire you to effectuate a change that is very important to them. While the discussion likely starts out with a review of the past and how that has led to a problem that now needs to be solved, your focus is on the imagined future and how the other person's life can be changed for the better. As David Bowie suggests, the passage of time, with proper reflection, can change the people you serve, and fixating on past events that are not relevant to helping the patient or client is a waste of time. In building Insta-Trust, you need to keep your eye on the ball of being future-oriented rather than discussing past matters that are not germane to problem solving.

Your listening approach needs to be oriented to problem solving for the person sitting next to you. Most people think they listen to others in an effort to understand what is truly on the other person's mind. But do you really listen to understand the other person or are you listening to confirm your perceived notions of the problem and the person? In other words, are you *really* looking to confirm what you think about the problem rather than discovering who is in front of you and how you can help them solve their problem? Most of us are "confirmation bias" junkies; you do not carefully listen to the other person, and when you respond to them, you do so in a manner that is consistent with your preconceived guess (and in many cases it is a premature guess) about the matter at hand.

Confirmation bias is dangerous on two levels. First, you are not always as smart as you think you are. You might have strong technical knowledge about the matter at hand, but your knowledge is not perfect; no one's is. The situation presented by a Patricia might be different in scope, complexity or actual technical requirements than matters you have previously handled. If you want to help others with their problems, however novel, you need to recognize that even the most mundane problem needs a fresh pair of eyes on it before rushing to tell the other person your proposed solution. Second, confirmation bias leads us to convey the impression to the other person that their deep concerns and comments are going into one of our ears and out the other without any care or concern. Potential clients can tell when you appear distracted or uninterested in what they are saying. They can tell when you are jumping the gun in terms of responding before a thorough discussion of what they are really saying.

The attitude of confirmation bias might be the most insidious element in our developing trusting relationships with potential clients. Listening for your own gratuitous benefit rather than for the benefit of the potential client is a trust killer. Such selfish listening also prevents you from providing the best possible advice or care to a client or patient. In the context of building trust in negotiations, failure to listen to understand the interests, the risk profile and the time elements of the other side prevents you from reaching an agreement that can successfully benefit you while also helping the other side. Stop rushing to judgment in terms of what you *think* is best for the other person and focus more on what *is* in their best interest.

Active listening requires your 100 percent attention to the client and their problem. When you are actively listening, you are trying to ascertain the issues that client brings to the surface and the issues that you sense might be lurking beneath the surface. You are not their therapist, their psychologist or their psychiatrist. However, you are listening at the outset of your conversation for one purpose and one purpose alone: to understand the other person as a human being and what the nature of their problem is.

"STOP RUSHING TO JUDGMENT IN TERMS OF WHAT YOU *THINK* IS BEST FOR THE OTHER PERSON AND FOCUS MORE ON WHAT *IS* IN THEIR BEST INTEREST."

Dr. Larry Jacobson

Active listening also involves listening to the nonverbal cues being presented by the other person. You need to pay close attention to the tone of their voice. You need to pay close attention to their eyes (if in person or by video conferencing). If you are meeting in person, you need to pay attention to their body language. Active listening is not just something observable through your ears; you also actively listen with your eyes as well. The nonverbal clues you observe can give you more information than the words spoken by the other person. A nervous voice can contradict words that suggest confidence. An excitable voice can suggest a degree of nervousness far greater than the words the client uses. Shrugged shoulders can demonstrate a lack of interest in what you are saying or how you are saying it. Pay close attention to their nonverbal cues and treat them as equal in importance to what they are saying.

Nonverbal cues that indicate a person's state of mind might include:

1. Voice tone.

2. Voice volume.

3. Pace of speech.

4. Eye contact or lack thereof.

5. Eye rolling.

6. Eyes that appear distant and uninterested.

7. Arm movement, such as arms folded, arms that are moving to make a point and arms that are stiff and rarely move.

8. If observable, whether the other person moves either in their chair or walking around in the room.

Many experts suggest the use of restating what the other person said in order to (1) show comprehension and (2) indicate that you are following the conversation with concentration. When used in a careful and clinical manner, restatements can be an effective tool for demonstrating to the other person that you are deeply interested in them and their problem. However, like most techniques, restating can be overused to the point that your restatements come off as robotic and as showing (contrary to your intent) that you are really more concerned about appearing to be an active listener than actually active listening. This is true with initial patient or client interactions, as well as during the negotiation process. Your objective is to pick and choose when the client says something that deserves your acknowledgment of their comments.

When you use restatement to demonstrate active listening, do it in a way that first acknowledges what the other person is saying. But then add a probing question after the restatement that moves the process forward in terms of ascertaining their intent. For example, in the case of a physician, after restating one of the concerns of a potential patient regarding a treatment plan, you might ask them about their previous experience committing to following medical advice after a diagnosis. If you are an attorney, after you acknowledge the potential client's objective, you might ask them about their risk profile, their time horizon or their non-financial interests. If you use restatements periodically to demonstrate your understanding of the client and their situation, and then build on those restatements to move the process forward in a way that helps the client see the bigger-picture aspect of the situation, you will build deep Insta-Trust in a relatively short period of time.

Unfortunately, active listening can be utilized in a manner that is destructive to building trust or solving client problems. A professional well versed in active listening can manipulate the questioning in a manner that is counterproductive to the client's best interest. If the patient says that they are afraid of anesthesia and surgery and there is an alternative nonsurgical approach that might give them an acceptable outcome, the surgeon should go through an active listening approach that at least gives the patient a fair assessment of the surgical and nonsurgical outcomes, even though the surgeon may not financially benefit from the nonsurgical approach. If dealing with a contested litigation matter, after going through an active listening process, you see a way to settle the matter quickly and in a way that benefits your client, your goal is not to keep the conversation going solely so that you can rack up the billable hours, but to lay out viable options that might be in the client's best interest.

Active listening, like any other tool used by a professional, has to be done through the prism of an ethical construct. You are not listening to manipulate or to achieve a preconceived goal in terms of representation. If you are an ethical active listener, your objective is to understand, as much as is humanly possible in an initial meeting, them as a human being, their problem and how their problem is negatively impacting them. Active listening, if done properly and ethically, is all about demonstrating to the potential client or patient that you really understand them on those three levels: the human level, the problem level and the impact level. You need to understand them on these levels AND they need to know you understand them on all three levels. Once you accomplish this, you have built deep trust, and then you can move to the active listening stage of problem solving. Think about one of your best outcomes and how you developed trust on a human level and on a technical level.

You are not a priest or a rabbi. No one is suggesting that you are so infallible that you never let financial or other material considerations enter your thought process with new clients or patients. You need to earn a living and cannot take on every worthy matter that might come across your desk. It is OK to acknowledge there is a financial element in much of what you do as a professional. But the financial element of your career is a function of the quality of your *perceived* ability to understand and assist clients with their difficult problems. If you use active listening solely for the purpose of gaining clients for financial gain, you are doing those clients great harm. Active listening is a tool that is for the client's benefit; any benefit you derive from active listening is derivative. Since the derivative financial benefits from being an ethical active listener are likely to be substantial, doing the right active listening approach will build trust in a far deeper manner than using active listening to manipulate a client to adopt an approach that might not be in their best interest.

"THE FINANCIAL ELEMENT OF YOUR CAREER IS A FUNCTION OF THE QUALITY OF YOUR *PERCEIVED* ABILITY TO UNDERSTAND AND ASSIST CLIENTS WITH THEIR DIFFICULT PROBLEMS."

Dr. Larry Jacobson

The use of stories is very helpful in an active listening context. If a potential client expresses a specific concern that you have dealt with before, do not hesitate to use a story about how you had a prior client with a similar situation (never say an identical situation with a prior client as that might make them feel you are not interested in THEIR problem) and how you assuaged their concerns prior to your representation. If you can show the client you are listening to and appreciating their concerns and have previous experience successfully resolving similar problems, you will go a long way toward building Insta-Trust.

Your goal is to listen in order to understand the other person as deeply as possible. By the end of your initial interaction, the appropriate use of active listening techniques will allow you to sit in the shoes of the potential client and determine what is likely in their best overall interest in terms of a solution or plan of action. Active listening is an interactive process in which you are having a natural conversation designed to draw out the spectrum of concerns about the problem at hand. The conversation has to feel natural and not as if you are making pronouncements from Mount Everest. They need to leave the conversation feeling that it had enough depth, comfortable with you as a person and knowing how you can help them solve a major problem. The great active listener comes off as a great conversationalist. If that is your lodestar, you will be viewed by others as a trustworthy professional.

Here is a personal story that shows that the patient and clinical use of active listening can result in establishing a strong professional relationship, even with a skeptical client.

Presently, I work with oral surgeons in a wide variety of settings. I represent buyers and sellers of practices. I work with practices in structuring employment contracts and partner buy-ins and buyouts. I work with them in their recruiting. I consult on major strategic planning such as evaluating financing options, opening additional offices and business expansion. I self-title myself as being their Turning Point Maven.

Selling a practice that you have run for 25 years or more is a gut-wrenching experience. The oral surgeon might retire for health reasons, to spend more time with family, to relocate, to move on to other professional challenges or a multitude of other reasons. Regardless of the reason, in almost every instance, the decision to sell is as much an emotional decision as a logical one. In any initial conversation with a prospective selling client, I understand that any meaningful discussion will have a component that is at least 50 percent emotional and somewhat less than 50 percent financial and process oriented.

I am picking one specific situation where an oral surgeon hired me to sell his practice. This seller was one tough dude. He was truly outstanding at his technical skills; I would go to him in a heartbeat if I needed a wisdom tooth removed or an implant inserted. At the outset of our initial conversation, he emphasized solely the financial aspects of a sale. He was interested in getting a specific price and was not interested in a penny less. He was willing to wait 6, 12 or even 18 months for the right buyer to acquire his practice. I listened to him for probably 15 to 20 minutes, taking notes and not saying a single word.

Once he finished, I asked him if it was OK to ask some questions; I generally find with challenging people it is best to ask first if it is OK to ask questions as it shows respect for their intellect and time. He said it was OK. I asked him a single question: "If I brought you a person who was interested in purchasing your practice who was clearly a misogynistic or bigoted person, would you sell your practice to that person if they met your sales price?" He responded in less than one second, "Of course not." My immediate response was, "Then price is not the sole criterion for selling your practice, and I need to spend a lot more time to get to really understand you." I asked him if I could ask a series of non-financial questions and he said yes.

So I spent the next half hour asking him questions, and here are some of those questions I asked (this type of questioning in terms of digging deep into the other person's past is an indicator of their present state of mind and can be used in many situations, even if the actual questions will differ based on context). I started with questions as to why he applied to oral surgery programs. Why did he decide to live and practice in his area? How did he manage balancing a family and a thriving practice? What trade-offs did he make? Did he regret any of those trade-offs? What would he say *was the greatest success of his career and what were his greatest regrets? If he was asked to give a one-sentence vision statement that incorporates the core of his professional being, what would that sentence be? And if he was asked to give a one-sentence vision statement that incorporates the core of his personal being, what would that sentence be?*

By the end of this process, we had a pretty full picture of this oral surgeon's personality. I then asked him if he wanted to ask me personal questions in order to get to know me better. He said he appreciated the opportunity and then spent the next 10 to 15 minutes asking me questions that focused on my personal and professional values. In particular, I found a way to emphasize that maximizing personal income was secondary to serving my clients in finding them the best possible transitional outcome. I gave him my professional mission statement that "I provide bespoke transition assistance to clients and put their needs over mine." Once we finished our respective personal disclosures, I then gave the prospective client a list of seven factors to use to evaluate a prospective purchaser. I asked him to put a percentage next to each factor so that adding up the seven factors would equal 100 percent. Clearly the sales price in his case (and this is true in most cases) has the highest percentage, but in this case (and after the personal discussion) the other six factors did add up to around 35 percent. After we finished the factor process, he hired me to sell his practice on the spot and we did end up selling his practice at a very nice price.

In this case, the seller appeared to be a methodical, rational professional. You can build a relationship by asking pertinent questions that seem to be slightly off point, but the purpose of the questions was to build trust and then a relationship. **The use of active listening is absolutely critical to developing a strong initial bond with a potential patient, client or negotiating counterparty; if they think you aren't listening, they think you don't care.**

WHEELS OF INSTA-TRUST™:
Willing Listeners

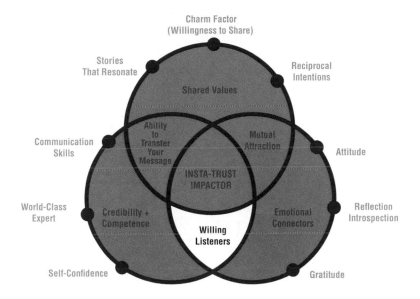

The ability to demonstrate you are a Willing Listener is a concept that applies to the ideas described in this chapter. Moving to the Credibility and Competence circle, the active listener is one who shows great competence and credibility through the use, not only of perceptive open-ended questions, but also strategic paraphrasing and asking questions that help the professional understand the other person's emotional, practical and latent goals. Willing Listening involves not only your actual understanding but also your communication to the potential client that you understand. Then moving to the intersecting Emotional Connectors circle, you show Willing Listening by demonstrating an eager-to-learn attitude coupled with gratitude that they have come to you as their potential problem solver. In order to be a great Willing Listener, you need to listen to understand, not to respond. Even more important, you need to listen to obtain a 360-degree assessment of the person and their problems, stated and unstated. You need a great technical background to do that, and as important, you need to dig deep to listen to who they really are and what personal and professional problems they need you to understand and solve.

Now on to the archetypes:

CLOSE-TO-THE-VEST. Active listening with the close-to-the-vest personality requires substantial patience. Since they are unlikely to volunteer much about themselves or their problem, you need to start your active listening process by asking a series of questions related to the personal/emotional aspect of the problem and then follow up with questions related to the problem itself and how it impacts them rationally. If they aren't clear in any of their answers, paraphrase and follow up to make sure that you fully understand them. By continuing to ask them pertinent questions, you are slowly building trust. Think of the long game.

THE TOUGH NUT. As a skeptic, the tough nut might be as challenging as the close-to-the-vest personality in terms of the sustained use of active questions. But there are some differences. First, observation of nonverbal cues such as voice tone and eye contact can be a form of active listening of a tough nut that can lead to clues as to how to get information and build trust. Second, by asking important questions, you can be frank with the tough nut that your approach is designed to challenge them to disclose matters of a personal and business nature that can help you help them. Paraphrasing, as long as it is not used to the extreme, is an effective tool with a tough nut. There is nothing wrong with being frank with a tough nut that your active and persistent questioning is designed to get to the bottom of their issue. The hope is that they recognize the reason for your mode of questioning, and you communicate it is not for your benefit, but their benefit.

THE KNOW-IT-ALL. When dealing with a know-it-all who doesn't know it all, your use of active questioning is not only designed to build a relationship and solve a problem, but to demonstrate in a subtle manner their lack of knowledge related to the subject matter. By using strategic and skilled questions and providing emotional support during the questioning process, you can demonstrate to the know-it-all that their knowledge base regarding the topic is weak and that you are there to lead them through a discussion of the real matters that need to be discussed. This type of active listening really requires a level of subtlety, as you are walking a fine line between guiding the potential client to rethinking their misguided viewpoint and having them realize they are being told they are wrong. While there may be times where you need to use active listening to explicitly call out the know-it-all, if there is no other way to get to the bottom of the problem, calling out a potential client should be the approach of last resort.

THE NOVICE. Active questioning of a novice client should be obvious. But do it in a sensitive manner. With the novice, explain up front that you are going to ask a lot of questions and that they will all be relevant to their situation. Explain that your follow-up questions are designed to clarify their answers. Periodically paraphrase their answers so they know you are doing this for their benefit. Don't hesitate to ask them occasionally if there are things you are discussing that are unclear. Active listening with a novice is a great way to build trust, but there is a fine line between asking questions that make the other person feel dumb for not knowing the answer and asking questions that appear to them to be helpful to their situation.

THE TIRE KICKER. With the tire kicker, you need to use more active questioning in the beginning of the conversation than normal since you are trying to ascertain whether they are serious about the problem and hiring you to solve it. Your questioning is as much about getting to their root emotional and practical concerns as it is seeing if this is someone you can develop a trusting relationship with. At some point, after you have asked a series of important questions and have followed up with a series of clarifying questions, it is fair game to ask the tire kicker as to whether they have any additional questions for you. By putting the burden on them to show that they are also actively listening, you can ascertain whether you want to continue with the conversation or think it is time to end it. There is nothing wrong with asking the tire kicker to make a decision; if you think the answer might be no, there is no reason to waste further time. If you think they might say maybe, ask a few more pertinent questions to see if you can move them off the point.

THE INDECISIVE. The indecisive falls somewhere close to the novice in terms of the use of active listening. If the client or patient is genuinely indecisive and shows an inclination to trust you personally and your ability to help them, you simply need to demonstrate a great deal of patience and ask them a lot of relevant personal questions. You then need to follow up on their answers with questions that build on their responses. That way they can see you really care about them and their problem. Then you can do the same approach when it comes to active questioning and listening during the problem-solving stage of the conversation. Continue to ask them if there is anything being discussed that is overly complicated or not understandable. Indicate you have as much time, within reason, to make them comfortable with you and the process. The indecisive may occasionally take advantage of your time, but most of the time they will deeply appreciate it when you show through active listening that you are trying to really figure them out.

THE LONG-TIMER. Your active listening protocol with the long-timer needs to be elastic, but within limits. The long-timer is looking for a long-term relationship and is using the discussion stage to evaluate you as a person and as a problem solver. So your questions need to be very much on point, and the strategic use of paraphrasing is important. The long-timer needs to see that you are truly interested in getting to know them as a person and that you want to become their problem solver. As with all conversations, you want to be in quiet control of the process and content, but with the long-timer, you might be more elastic in terms of adapting your questions to their long-term orientation. With the genuine long-timer, the active questioner who acts like a tortoise wins the race.

THE SCHMOOZER. With the schmoozer, you should use active listening as an important trust-building tool, but within limits. You need to keep the conversation on point and, as stated previously, be in command of the conversation and process. When the conversation goes seriously off track, you need to be gently frank with the schmoozer that you can have off-topic conversations at a later time (hopefully never) but for now and their benefit, both of you need to stay on track and get their issue on the table. Most schmoozers, when gently confronted with an explanation of staying on point, will understand the need to get down to business. With a schmoozer, don't be afraid to be explicit that you are engaging in an active listening process and that the process is designed solely for the purpose of helping them. You can build trust with a schmoozer by calling out your process and showing empathy while you are engaging in an active listening exercise.

THE KNOWLEDGEABLE. Perhaps the easiest archetype to engage in active listening exercises, the knowledgeable responds to clear questions and appreciates it when you clearly demonstrate an understanding of what they are telling you. But don't forget to start with some active questioning at the outset about their pain point and underlying concerns. Emotionally driven active questioning and listening can demonstrate to even the most logical and knowledgeable client that you are treating them and their problem as an integrated situation. Active listening that shows you are attentive to the knowledgeable's personal concerns can make the problem-solving question part of the conversation go more smoothly. With the knowledgeable, you have to show your A-game in terms of active questioning and listening, because they will be at the top of their game when they ask you deep questions that are based off their prior experiences.

THE QUICK DRAW. The tendency with quick draws is to minimize the conversation, especially those that involve active listening. While some reduction in conversation length is OK (and by not dragging things out the way you would with the long-timer), coming off as rushed in terms of your questioning and your acknowledgment of their concerns (personal and technical) does not help your cause. Be very precise in your questioning and allow them to follow up since they are not likely to waste your time. Be judicious in your paraphrasing to only important matters. Be professional and respect their time and they will respect yours. Being respectful of their time will build trust. But don't shortcut the need to ask sufficient questions in terms of quantity and quality; trust can happen quickly, but you still have to do the legwork to show you care about the person and their problem.

THE EGOMANIAC. The egomaniac might find active questioning a bore because he or she might feel that you are getting all touchy-feely with them since it is always only about them and their ego. So when you engage in active questioning and listening with the egomaniac, ask your questions with an edgy tone so they can hear that you are subtly demonstrating mastery over the process (meaning the conversation) and the direction of the conversation. Acknowledge their position and (where appropriate) knowledge base and indicate that you take their situation very seriously.

Communicate that you want to get to work immediately and you are the right person to solve their problem. Ask a few questions that massage their ego. Then move quickly into a discussion of the problem. Your questions, tone and body language should focus on showing a high degree of attentiveness as you explain how you perceive the problem as it impacts THEM. When you're active listening with egomaniacs, always make it clear that you are following everything they say with razor-like concentration. That is what they are used to from their sycophants. But never lose control of the questioning and the conversation. If you do, you will lose the respect of the egomaniac and the ability to help them.

Ask Yourself

QUESTION ONE. Am I a confirmation-bias problem analyzer?

QUESTION TWO. Do I listen to understand the other person or do I listen to respond to them?

QUESTION THREE. When I actively listen, am I concentrating not only on their actual words, but on the subtext of what they are trying to communicate?

QUESTION FOUR. In my active listening, am I also focusing on voice tone and, where possible, their eye contact and body language?

QUESTION FIVE. Am I strategic in my paraphrasing during my active listening and questioning process?

QUESTION SIX. Do I use follow-up questions as a means to not only obtain more pertinent information from the other person, but to demonstrate I am problem solving for their benefit?

QUESTION SEVEN. Does my active listening style come off as a natural conversation as opposed to seeming like an interrogation?

|INTERLUDE|

"WHO ARE YOU?"
(COURTESY OF PETE TOWNSHEND)

How well do you really know yourself? If you had to choose, which one (or more) of the 11 archetypes in this book might you be characterized as? What is your real empathy style? How well do you read people's personalities? How good of an active listener are you? How good are you at collaborative problem solving?

A critical message to take out of this book in terms of how to build Insta-Trust with a potential patient or client is, KNOW THYSELF BEFORE YOU ATTEMPT TO KNOW OTHERS. By knowing your own personality and how the strengths and weaknesses of that personality type might interact with someone else whose personality type is entirely different, you allow yourself to modify your dominant personality characteristics accordingly. For example, my personality tends toward the knowledgeable, the quick draw and, in a number of cases, the tough nut. People with those types of personality traits can be impatient, dominant in conversations, and can make assumptions that the potential client or patient knows more about the issue and their emotions related to the issue than actually is the case. As such, I need to modulate my behavior to come off as far less dominant in terms of displaying my expertise and the tone in which I conduct the conversation. I need to spend more time working on the interpersonal aspects of relationship building early in the conversation. I also need to be a better active listener on all fronts, i.e., questions, paraphrasing and observations of nonverbal cues. The point is, I am honest enough (I hope) about my weaknesses to continue to work on them in order to build Insta-Trust with potential clients.

You should do a hard self-assessment of your personality traits. Which of the archetypes described in this book fit you? The likelihood is several of the archetypes apply to you, at least in certain settings. How do you use your archetypes to your advantage and the advantage of the Patricias who come to you for solutions? Which of the archetypes cause you to be less effective than you could be with the Patricias who come to you for solutions? How can you reduce the negative elements of your personality in order to show client-centeredness in your interactions with the Patricias of your world? One way to assess your strengths and weaknesses is to have five individuals whose insight you truly admire and who have seen you in action in terms of conversations in new or novel settings give you an honest assessment of your skill set in the areas of conversational trust building, demonstrating an interest in the other person during a conversation, your active listening skills and your collaborative problem-solving skills. Ask them what archetypes you present to others. Meet with them in person; individuals tend not to be as truthful on sensitive issues when the communication is via text, email or even phone. Plan for the meeting to be at least 60 minutes and be prepared to take notes in order to learn from the interaction and to show the other person (who is doing you a great favor) that you are actively listening and taking their evaluation seriously. Ask them to be brutally honest, and in no case attempt to rebut their observations. If there are areas where you are unclear, it is OK to ask clarifying questions, the same way you would if you were having an active listening and questioning conversation. At the end of the conversation, thank them and reciprocate by offering them the opportunity to assist them on a matter of importance to them in the future.

Your self-observation involves assessing your character. Your character is what shows to potential clients or patients. The strength of your character is your greatest asset during your initial interaction with a client and during the course of your representation. But there is a second element of your persona that is as important as your self-reflection. That is your private and public reputation.

Your character describes who you are. Your reputation describes how other people view your character. You can be the most competent professional in your niche and have the best trust-building toolkit, but if your reputation is the opposite, it really does not matter how talented you are, how empathetic you are and what a great active listener you are. In this world, for better or worse, you are as good as your public reputation. So once you truly understand yourself and how your personality gels with others, then you need to move outside your self-reflection and focus on how others see you.

Given social media, reviews on Yelp or Google and reviews on websites that allow for comments on how well professionals dealt with patients or clients on a spectrum of concerns, potential clients or patients have a wealth of information regarding your performance and bedside manner. The information might not always be accurate and the reviewer might have ulterior motives for giving a negative review. But the stark reality is that potential clients have a lot more information regarding you than you will ever be able to get about them in a limited period of time prior to an initial interaction.

Your reputation is as vital an asset as any money you have in the bank. Many older professionals tend to give short shrift to concern about their reputation on social media or the Internet. Their view is that the people who work with them, their prior clients and their professional network know how well they solve problems and interact with clients. Thus, these professionals take the position that their "silent reputation" is more important than the raucous and Wild West posts on the Internet. These professionals have a very short-sighted view of the current world of reputation management.

In today's world, professionals cannot rely simply on their silent reputation to precede them in terms of client expectations prior to an initial interaction. Yes, having a great silent reputation helps when the client who is getting ready to meet you is getting a referral from another professional. But more and more, potential clients are taking a proactive approach to doing their due diligence on their prospective professionals. Some potential clients might be connected enough to have an informal network they can tap into to find out about your trustworthiness and technical skill level. Most will rely on social media postings and Internet reviews to make initial assessments of you, for better or worse.

You need to constantly monitor your reputation online. If you have the staff to do so, you should have someone respond with gratitude to positive reviews or posts. If someone posts a negative review, it makes little sense to respond to their review explaining yourself or arguing as to why they are wrong. Rather, acknowledge their feelings and offer to have a private conversation with them about what you could have done better (and if you have that conversation, just sit back and listen to them without rebuttal).

One way to enhance your online reputation is to have client testimonials on your website and, if you use social media outlets such as Facebook, Twitter, LinkedIn or Instagram, post them on those sites. It is even better if those testimonials are in video form, as the prospective client can see and hear the excellent things the satisfied client has to say about you. Video resonates far better in terms of helping you burnish your reputation than reading something on a screen. Having others, preferably a diversity of others in terms of demographics, testify as to how much you listened to them and handled their situation with a high degree of sensitivity provides you with a level of reputation that can overcome the random negative review in a social media or Internet post. And as stated earlier, making prior successful patients or clients available to speak with a prospective client shows a level of quiet confidence in your trustworthiness and skill level that can overcome the social media trolls.

Finally, you can be proactive in building a social media reputational profile if your professional service firm allows it. What social media format do you feel most comfortable using? Use platforms that are frequented by your target Patricias. For some professionals, it might be blogging. For some, it might be Twitter or LinkedIn. For others, it might be posting educational videos on YouTube that show you, in a calm and soothing manner, educating prospective clients about some of the matters you handle.

Subconsciously, if potential clients see that you are trustworthy enough to help plenty of others, you are off to a good start for your initial conversation. Other ways of building an online reputational profile include blogging, sending periodic newsletters, posting nontechnical information about what you are working on (within the bounds of confidentiality and professional ethics) and posting targeted social media content. For many professionals, Facebook or Instagram might not be the optimal place for your postings (and depending on their policies it might be viewed as advertising that you need to pay for), but in some professional niches Facebook and Instagram might be a good way to reach your target audience. For many professionals, LinkedIn might be a good vehicle for periodic postings that demonstrate both your technical knowledge and your professional demeanor. You should figure out what online method can best get your reputational profile its largest and most engaged audience. You need to target for breadth and depth of your potential client base.

So...who are you?

You should know your character, and if you don't, you better get other trustworthy colleagues to give you a candid assessment. You can control a good part, although not all, of your private reputation among colleagues, former patients or clients, or your professional network. You cannot control much of your public reputation. Your objective is to control as much of your online reputatation as you possibly can. Many professionals might find online reputation management distatesful; however, it is a necessary element of professional branding and client development. So when asked, "Who are you?" would you rather have (frequently) nameless disgruntled persons controlling your online reputation or take the bull by the horns and create your own online reputational persona? If you know yourself, you know the answer.

"YOUR REPUTATION IS AS VITAL AN ASSET AS ANY MONEY YOU HAVE IN THE BANK."

– Dr. Larry Jacobson

"KNOW THYSELF BEFORE YOU ATTEMPT TO KNOW OTHERS."

Dr. Larry Jacobson

TRUST BUILDING 104: CREATE AN IDEA THAT LEADS TO A MUTUALLY AGREED UPON SOLUTION

"A fanatic is one who can't change his mind and won't change the subject."
— Winston Churchill

You likely identify yourself as a professional who works in a narrow specialty. If you are a dermatologist, you view yourself as someone who works with skin disease. If you are an investment banker or a broker, you view yourself as someone who represents buyers or sellers of companies or real estate. If you are an attorney, depending on your specialty, you view yourself as someone who practices a specific type of law.

With all due respect, your professional designation is impressive, but your real life work is as a PROBLEM SOLVER. You are not an academic who teaches the underlying skill set of your profession. You are not a researcher whose sole job is to expand the knowledge base of professionals in your field. No, you are working with real-life human beings, with real-life problems that are causing real-life issues and (in many instances) real pain. Your potential clients and patients come to you to help them with a very specific problem. Once you get beyond the trust-building stage with the potential client, your job is to diagnose their real problem and come up with appropriate potential solutions. As the Churchill quote above suggests, if you identify as a professional solely based on your specialty, you might come off to a potential client as a fanatic who is more impressed with yourself than the person sitting in front of you or on the phone with you.

"YOUR PROFESSIONAL DESIGNATION IS IMPRESSIVE, BUT YOUR REAL LIFE WORK IS AS A PROBLEM SOLVER."

Dr. Larry Jacobson

During the initial Insta-Trust conversation, there is a limit as to how much diagnosis and fact-finding you can achieve. In fact, as professionals, one has to be careful about diagnosing an issue and recommending a firm solution. Yes, there are many situations where the real problem and diagnosis can take place in the initial meeting; such examples are if a wisdom tooth needs to be removed, if it is clear that the patient needs a knee replacement, if the IRS audit letter has been received and the client needs a CPA. In situations like these, you can come up with a broad recommendation to the client as to how to proceed. However, in many situations, the development of a fully crystalized idea might take a significant amount of time, so the professional needs to first come up with a "pre-solution" in order to make the client feel comfortable with the professional (both the relationship and their abilities) and then once hired, delve deeply into problem-solving mode.

One needs to have a high skill level in terms of relationship development to be able to get the potential client to hire them prior to the recommendation of a very specific course of action. In fact, one thing that can destroy trust and reputation is when a professional thinks that they can offer a concrete solution to a problem without a full investigation of the issues involved. For example, in the area of anesthesia, there is a reason why their preoperative questioning is so extensive; various health issues can impact the type and amount of anesthesia used in a surgical procedure. And if the answers given are incomplete or inaccurate, people can die (one of my clients had a patient whose referring physician gave an incomplete medical history to my client and the patient died because they could not tolerate the type of anesthesia used based on the incomplete medical history).

There is nothing worse in terms of professional reputation than a shoot-from-the-hip advisor. Yes, there are many situations where the professional can make a quick assessment (such as my knee replacement) and come up with a concrete idea, or several, that can help the prospective client. In those situations, during the initial Insta-Trust meeting, the professional should feel comfortable, after the trust-building stage and the fact-finding stage, coming up with a specific idea that meets the client's needs on every different level (whether those needs involve material, physical, emotional or other concerns). Let's take a moment to discuss the "ideal idea."

A client concern often has a surface (obvious) component but sometimes has an underlying component that is not very obvious until the professional digs down to figure out the various latent concerns that the potential client is unable to volunteer. Therefore, the professional must spend the requisite amount of time with the potential client asking questions that relate to both the surface and latent concerns. This is a delicate balancing act. On the one hand, you really need data (hard and soft) in order to generate client-oriented solutions. On the other hand, the client shouldn't feel like they are going through an inquisition in terms of a gauntlet of questions. So how do you handle this dance? You should ask a few questions and then pause to state the reasoning behind that line of questioning. Then you ask the prospective client what questions they have in terms of why you're going down that line of inquiry. Even during the fact-finding portion of the conversation, the Insta-Trust oriented professional tries to keep the conversation as personal and nontechnical as possible. When you are dealing with a fellow professional (such as in-house counsel or accountants, staff physicians or fellow deal makers), it is acceptable to speak at a highly technical level, but when you are speaking with someone who is not a fellow expert in your area, it is vitally important that the other person feel you are talking with them and not to them.

Your goal during the fact-finding stage of the conversation is twofold. The first is obvious: to gain enough information to give the potential client an idea of how you will assist them with their problem. The second goal is more subtle: to build further and deeper trust with the potential client. What separates the novice trust builder from the expert trust builder is that the expert understands that every element of the conversation from start to finish not only has a technical component (meaning finding out the client's problem and coming up with solutions), but a relationship-building component. You can start out with a great relationship-building beginning of your conversation and totally destroy that goodwill by clumsily handling the fact-finding part of the conversation. You need to really focus on the potential client as you are asking fact-finding questions.

A good fact finder is an active listener. You ask questions, in as nontechnical a manner as possible, and once you receive an answer, you ask a follow-up question that (1) builds on the answer given and (2) leads the conversation naturally to further inquiries that could be highly relevant in terms of coming up with a client-oriented solution. To the extent humanly possible, the questioning should seem like a natural conversation and the potential client should feel like they are engaged in an expansion of the relationship-building part of the conversation. Clients feel more comfortable working with professionals who treat them as equal partners in the solution-finding process than professionals who talk down to them. In fact, my doctoral dissertation research found that the number one element that created distrust between the parties was the persona of talking down to the other side.

During the conversational fact-finding stage, if the matter is complex and not subject to an immediate, firm potential solution, your goal is to get as much information as possible so you can develop one or more tentative solutions to present to the client (or in negotiation, the other side). As much as you might like to shoot from the hip, don't. In situations without an obvious solution, your default approach (when appropriate) should be to try to develop multiple potential tentative solutions to present to the client or other negotiator. There are several reasons why presenting multiple potential solutions provides an optimal approach. First, it demonstrates you have been carefully listening to the potential client (or other side in a negotiation) and have quickly developed a solution mindset that will help them in the future. Even if none of those solutions are ultimately implemented, the fact that you showed enough skill to quickly come up with bona fide solutions will build trust and result in a potential future representation or solution. Second, coming up with multiple solutions gives the parties the future opportunity to drill down to the pros and cons of each approach as to their effectiveness and, if necessary, for future refinement. Third, the multiple-potential-solution approach shows the client (or other negotiating party) the excellence of your technical skills. Showing that you are a skillful professional and have an action-oriented solution mindset is also an important part of building Insta-Trust. You can be the best interpersonal professional in the world, but ultimately you have to deliver the goods in terms of being damn good at what you do. Quick development of client-oriented solutions shows you as the ultimate Insta-Trust Impactor. The Insta-Trust Impactor builds relational and technical trust with potential clients.

"YOU CAN BE THE BEST INTERPERSONAL PROFESSIONAL IN THE WORLD, BUT ULTIMATELY YOU HAVE TO DELIVER THE GOODS IN TERMS OF BEING DAMN GOOD AT WHAT YOU DO."

Dr. Larry Jacobson

When presenting potential solutions to prospective clients in an initial conversation, make sure your ideas meet all of their known and latent (to the extent you can discover those in an initial meeting) needs. An idea that solely helps with surface needs may result in a short-term gain but not a long-term benefit to the potential client. When I saw the orthopedic surgeon, he made it clear that there were short-term solutions to my knee replacement (such as cartilage injections) but that those solutions were band-aids for what ultimately would have to be done. Now there might have been a bona fide personal reason to take the short-term solution and delay the knee replacement, and the surgeon would have been perfectly fine with that approach. The critical point is that he offered multiple options based on what he knew of my physical problem, pain level and ability to do the post-surgical rehab. His options were not just based on an X-ray or the report of my non-surgical orthopedic specialist. His recommendations were based on an evaluation of my knee and my personal outlook. When developing ideas in an initial meeting, please take the time to discover whether there are latent concerns that could impact the recommendations you are about to make.

While your goal is to come up with a concrete idea or ideas that might clearly assist the client in accomplishing their objective, you have to be realistic that such a concrete idea does not always result from the initial meeting with the potential client. In fact, one of the key characteristics of an Insta-Trust Impactor is that he or she tactfully demonstrates to a client that their initial meeting went well, but there is a lot more work to be done to professionally to solve the client's problem. There is a delicate balance between a client feeling you are dragging out the process in an effort to get hired and legitimately needing more information and time to develop a client-oriented solution. Many potential clients, especially nonexpert clients, frequently expect that you can come up with quick solutions based on incomplete information and are very disappointed when, as a matter of professional analysis, you are unable to provide that quick solution.

The key to assuaging the potential client's fears is to be quite clear as to the additional information you will need to make a concrete recommendation and the process for obtaining that information. Make it clear to them that you would love to be able to give them a firm solution that will meet all of their needs, but that the situation is far too complicated for a seat-of-the-pants solution that may cause them more harm than good. Explain that caring professionals need to carefully examine problems like theirs from multiple angles after gaining all the facts. These explanations should be done in a manner that demonstrates you want to do the right thing for the potential client, even if it takes a while. Every element of advice giving during the solution portion of the conversation should be done from the perspective as to how you can convince the client that your solution(s) are designed solely in terms of their best interest.

"IF YOU CAN CONVINCE THEM YOUR SOLUTIONS ARE BASED SOLELY ON THEIR BEST INTEREST AND NOT YOUR POCKETBOOK, YOU HAVE A GREAT CHANCE OF BEING RETAINED BY THE CLIENT TO ASSIST THEM WITH THEIR PROBLEM."

– Dr. Larry Jacobson

WHEELS OF INSTA-TRUST™:
Credibility + Competence

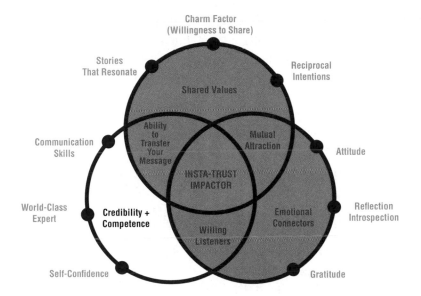

The ability to demonstrate Credibility and Competence is a concept that applies to the ideas described in this chapter. In order to create a mutually agreeable solution, you need to be able to deliver the goods. As demonstrated on the wheel, you need to be world-class at what you do. People who come to you for professional assistance are looking for a bespoke solution that meets their personal, professional and emotional needs. However, having world-class skills is far from enough. Having excellent communication skills, as the wheel requires, is not enough. You need to reinforce your skill level with a self-confident persona that leads others to gravitate toward you. If I were to say there is a single goal you should take from this book, it is to develop a blend of technical competence and emotional connection skills that cause others to gravitate toward you. If you are viewed by others as having the type of skills and personalities that allow them to naturally gravitate toward you, then by force of nature, your skills will be eagerly sought by individuals far and wide.

In wrapping up this chapter, your professional reputation requires a client-centered solution orientation. You are hired to come up with client-oriented solutions that work. Sometimes finding the solution can happen quickly. Much of the time, the determination of an optimal solution takes more time than the potential client expects. Your job is to manage the potential client's expectations if the solution development process requires deliberation. You do that through conversational fact-finding, digging deep into hidden issues and motives and giving preliminary solutions. The key is that the potential client can see, hear and feel that you are working hard before you are even retained to a problem-solving approach that is centered on them. The key concept to take out of this chapter is you will be hired when the potential client FEELS you are the right person to help them ultimately solve their problem. Your idea generation approach must take into account how your recommendations are received by the potential client from a logical, but especially an emotional standpoint. You don't want to come off as the type of fanatic described by Churchill; change your idea generation approach to meet the client where they need to be.

CLOSE-TO-THE-VEST. Idea creation with close-to-the-vest clients frequently requires a longish process, but not always. Some close-to-the-vest clients are reluctant to give out information regarding their goals during the information-gathering process, but many of this archetype are willing to share information if the process used by the professional is targeted to that which is needed to find a potential solution. The close-to-the-vest client does not like to waste time but respects professionals who appear to be focused on doing their jobs in a clinical matter. Idea generation may or may not take a while with a close-to-the-vest person; your best approach is to be matter-of-fact in terms of the how and why of your approach with them.

THE TOUGH NUT. As a skeptic, the tough nut is likely to want to take an active role in the idea generation part of the conversation. The tough nut is likely to want to have an extended conversation about why you are going through a particular line of questioning. They are likely to want to thoroughly discuss each potential idea you bring up as to the pros and cons. They will not be shy about their views of your recommendations. Your job is first and foremost to not let them hijack the process and conversation. But assuming you can keep control, the best way to deal with a tough nut is to let them, within reason, ask their questions. View this as an opportunity to gain their trust and learn about alternative solutions that you might not have thought about. When you present your potential ideas, make sure they listen to all of them first before you initiate a discussion of the pros and cons, which they will want to have. Most importantly, be quite firm in your support of your ideas, because coming off as ambivalent is about the worst thing you can do with a tough nut in terms of gaining their trust.

THE KNOW-IT-ALL. Like the tough nut, they are likely to have an extended conversation about why you are going through a particular line of questioning. However, your response should be different. With the know-it-all, your questioning should be designed not only to generate data and potential solutions, but to subtly show off your expertise. The know-it-all needs to discover, no later than the questioning stage, that they don't know all the facts regarding the issue. They need to be educated about the potential idea(s) you recommend, so patience might be required in explaining the "why" of your recommendation(s).

THE NOVICE. Idea generation will be tough for the novice, as while they might have a good sense of what the problem is, they will have little sense of what the potential solutions might be (unless they were told by someone else ahead of time of a potential solution to the problem). There is a tendency of professionals to speak down to the novice during the idea and solution portion of the conversation. DON'T DO IT. If there is only one likely solution to the problem, explain it in confident language and explain the likelihood that the solution will (or won't) fix the problem. Novices are more interested in the solution, so spend the time you might dedicate to idea generation with some of the other archetypes explaining the solution with sensitivity, knowledge (again, do not speak down to the person) and quiet confidence. As with the know-it-all, please explain the "why" of your approach to the novice, but unlike the know-it-all, the novice may not need a long explanation of the "how" of your approach.

You will build Insta-Trust with a novice when they feel you spent the right amount of time diagnosing the issue and coming up with a solution, even if it is a tentative solution that requires more investigation.

THE TIRE KICKER. With the tire kicker, their ambivalence about you (which in many instances has nothing to do with you and everything to do with them) really comes through during the fact gathering/idea generation stage. Your job is to keep their interest and determine whether the problem is serious and whether they are serious. There is nothing wrong during this stage with asking pointed questions about the matter in order to determine their commitment level to the process and your retention. You should ask about their commitment directly by asking how committed they might be to implementing your recommended solution. After giving out potential solutions, if they are finally convinced that you are the right person for the job, their implicit and explicit commitment should surface. If not, move on.

THE INDECISIVE. The truly indecisive potential client needs to be dealt with very carefully during the questioning/idea generation stage. Their indecision is not necessarily due to their concerns about you as an individual, although that could play a role. Their indecision often has to do with whether their pain level (personal or professional) is high enough that they are willing to make a commitment to doing something about their problem. Your role during the idea generation stage is to use your questioning and brainstorming to convince them the problem is of sufficient gravity that it requires their immediate attention. You need to convince them, through the quality of your questioning, that you care about their problem and are going through an intensive process in order to get them to see, not only your technical excellence, but your commitment to them as a person. At the end of your solution presentation, the best approach is to ask the indecisive whether they have any questions, and once those have been answered, be direct in asking them whether they are willing to move forward with you.

THE LONG-TIMER. With the long-timer, you might not even get to complete the idea generation stage during your initial meeting. They might want to use that meeting primarily, if not exclusively, to size you up as a person and determine whether or not you can be trusted at an interpersonal level. Do not be surprised if they ask for a follow-up meeting to discuss various courses of action. If they make this request, do not be offended, as it is a very good sign that they might permanently continue the relationship. However, if you do get into the fact-finding/idea generation stage during your initial conversation, please give the long-timer plenty of time to ask questions and make sure your questioning of them is targeted to the answers they give you as an active listener. Of all of the archetypes (along with the knowledgeable), the long-timers will be razor-focused on your ability to deeply understand them, their problem and bespoke solutions to their problem. Make the long-timer feel you are their trusty partner on an enduring journey.

THE SCHMOOZER. During the fact-finding and idea stage, you need to keep complete control of the situation. Frolics and detours are time wasters, but more importantly, with the schmoozer, take valuable time away from finding out important facts and latent concerns that might help you come up with their most optimal solution(s). Crisp questioning and careful answering of their relevant (and only relevant) questions is the best approach to not only gaining the trust of the schmoozer, but getting hired. Most schmoozers respect professionals who try to keep the conversation on the narrow after initial pleasantries. Keep the conversation natural and on point and you might find the schmoozer to be very cooperative during the idea generation process.

THE KNOWLEDGEABLE. The knowledgeable thrives on the idea generation stage of your initial meeting. Part of it involves ego on the part of the knowledgeable. But you need to be secure enough in your own ego and skill set to realize that the knowledgeable might come up with ideas that you have not thought of. In such a case, acknowledge the quality of the idea and show your respect and technical competence by thoroughly brainstorming the idea. On the other hand, if their proposed idea has little merit, do not shoot it down immediately. Interact with them and guide them toward seeing for themselves that the idea does not fit their needs. If the knowledgeable does not come up with potential solutions during the meeting, your job is to generate at least two or three ideas that could plausibly help their situation and then brainstorm those ideas as if you were colleagues. The best way to build Insta-Trust with a knowledgeable is for them to leave the meeting feeling like they were speaking and creative problem solving with a peer.

THE QUICK DRAW. You should expect the quick draw to want to prematurely move forward past the fact-finding and idea generation part of the process. They tend to be impatient and are looking for a fast response and a fast solution, regardless of whether that might be in their best interest. The Insta-Trust professional needs to slow down the quick draw and be firm about their information gathering and data analysis process. Of course, you can speed up the conversation if you are quickly getting what you need to come up with for excellent idea generation. But that decision is to be made by the professional, not the quick draw. You need to reassure the quick draw during the conversation that you are working expeditiously to find out the issues and developing tentative solutions. By asking them for some level of patience during this part of the process and then telling them you are respecting their patience level, you can develop a higher level of trust. Sometimes with a quick draw you gain more respect by acknowledging their personality and keeping the questioning to the bare minimum of what you need to make informed recommendations.

THE EGOMANIAC. This archetype needs to have their ego stroked by believing that they are responsible for at least 50 percent of the solution process. Their ego requires them to think that any solution you come up with is due, either explicitly or implicitly, to their contribution to the conversation. Your role is to not explicitly acknowledge their egocentric nature during the fact-finding or idea generation process, but to give them constant assurance that their comments are very helpful to you. In other words, to an extent, you will need to stroke their ego. However, you should not shortchange the process in terms of your fact-finding or professional analysis because the egomaniac will call you out if you don't appear to be 100 percent focused on them and their problem. When giving them your proposed solutions, be upfront in terms of giving them the opportunity to ask questions and test your analysis. The egomaniac can be your friend if you allow them to demonstrate their knowledge, but be firm if you think any of their approaches are off-base or run counter to their best interests. At the end of the day, professionally express your opinions to the egomaniac; they should respect you, but if they don't, move on.

Now that we have set forth the 11 archetypes and how they impact trust building with different personality types, please go to www.insta-trust.com for a free personality quiz on which archetypes best describe your personality.

Ask Yourself

QUESTION ONE. Is my idea generation approach motivated solely by a problem-solving mentality?

QUESTION TWO. Do I make a conscious effort not to shoot from the hip during the fact-finding and idea generation process?

QUESTION THREE. Do I acknowledge the limitations of fact-finding during an initial client meeting and make sure *only* to give recommendations that are based on solid analysis?

QUESTION FOUR. In my search for client-focused solutions, do I dig for their latent concerns?

QUESTION FIVE. Am I a conversational fact finder and idea generator?

QUESTION SIX. When I get to the idea presentation stage, do I think of multiple solutions when appropriate?

QUESTION SEVEN. Throughout the process, am I educating the potential client that follow-up meetings might be necessary to ascertain additional facts and develop more appropriate solutions?

BONUS QUESTION. When necessary, do I use the fact-finding and idea generation stage to move the client to hire me even though the initial conversation may not reveal a specific solution to their problem?

"YOU WILL BE HIRED WHEN THE POTENTIAL CLIENT FEELS YOU ARE THE RIGHT PERSON TO HELP THEM ULTIMATELY SOLVE THEIR PROBLEM."

Dr. Larry Jacobson

|10|

TRUST BUILDING 105:
EGO, THE VILLAIN THAT PREVENTS
INSTA-TRUST. HOW'S YOURS?

"Ego is the Enemy."
– Ryan Holiday

In many respects, the most important chapter is this last one. The role of ego in building trust plays a significant role in whether you will or will not be able to build Insta-Trust with potential clients and patients. To paraphrase Ryan Holiday, ego really is the enemy of your building long-term trusting relationships with clients that really could use your assistance. Ego destroys relationships before they get off the ground. Ego prevents others from seeing how you can really help them. I can tell you from personal experience that ego is an insidious disease that blocks the ability to develop new professional relationships. Previously, I rushed through the "getting to know you" stage with a new client. I would show impatience by interrupting them and asking technical questions above their knowledge base. I would show little empathy for those whose problems were meaningful but whose personalities were not pleasant. And I would assume all new clients had similar personality types; it took me a long time to figure out that my strategy in dealing with clients depended in significant part on the archetype or archetype categories they represented.

The disease of ego prevents you from having the ability to serve others at a very high skill level.

"WHAT GOOD IS IT FOR YOU TO BE THE BEST PROFESSIONAL IN YOUR NICHE IF NO ONE WANTS TO WORK WITH YOU?"

Dr. Larry Jacobson

Once you reach a high level of professional competence, for many, you take on the mindset that you are the smartest person in the room. There is nothing you do not know. There is nothing new you can be told about your area. You engage in no self-reflection and do not monitor your skill set. In other words, you are the expert, damn it, and everyone needs to listen to what you are saying.

The difficulty is that ego frequently manifests itself with others in indirect and subtle ways. It is the rare professional who is so arrogant to actually say to a client that he or she knows what he is talking about and they need to listen to him or her. Rarely does a professional come out and engage in a lengthy brag fest. Rarely will a professional use colorful language to tell a prospective client that they are full of crap. Yes, all of this happens on occasion, and when it does, it is a very rare prospective client who will end up hiring the demonstrably arrogant professional. You and I want to work with professionals who are highly competent and confident.

"NO ONE WANTS TO WORK WITH THOSE WHO COME OFF AS PRIMA DONNAS."

– Dr. Larry Jacobson

Most of the time, arrogance comes off in far more subtle ways. The professional tends to lecture the patient rather than present himself or herself as collaborative. The professional interrupts the client/patient when they are speaking. The professional spends an inordinate amount of time talking about the other matters they have handled, not in order to show the client how those situations help frame potential solutions for this client, but to demonstrate their technical prowess. Finally, subtle arrogance gets conveyed through the use of nonverbal communication, such as finger tapping, exasperation in voice tone and moving the process along faster than what is necessary.

What good is it for you to be the best professional in your niche if no one wants to work with you?

One easy way that you can eliminate subtle arrogance and power moves in an initial interaction with a new client is to introduce yourself with your full name and then enthusiastically ask them to call you by your first name. Doing this not only puts the other person at ease, but subconsciously tells the new client you are approachable and want to interact with them on an equal plane. Also, make it clear very early in the conversation that the other person can feel comfortable if they don't understand or need clarification about anything you are saying that they should immediately stop the conversation and ask their question.

Subtle ego moves need to be acknowledged by you and eliminated. You need to have a collaborative mindset when speaking to a Patricia. It is fine to give technical explanations of what you are contemplating, but do it in a language that your prospect understands and give them plenty of opportunity to ask clarifying questions. Explain similar cases, but do it in a way that explicitly ties those matters back to how that will help the potential client. And by all means, observe yourself carefully in terms of the ways you demonstrate impatience in client interactions. You would be surprised by how often you convey through your body language and tone an impatience with potential (and actual) clients. Ego can be shown as much through the display of impatience (by word or other cues) than the most arrogant rant.

The next subtle ego impression you need to get rid of is giving the impression that you are the smartest person in the room. How does that manifest itself? First, by using overly technical explanations without regard to the comprehension level of the potential client. Second, by limiting the time the client has available for asking questions that are important to them. Third, by not fully answering their important questions that come up during the interpersonal and fact-finding parts of the conversation (it is OK to periodically state you will address a valid concern later and actually do so). Fourth, by coming across as if their problem is not serious. If they are coming to you, the problem is serious to them; if the problem is not truly serious, professionally say so and explain why and gently end the meeting.

The rest of this chapter will focus on ways you can develop strategies to check your ego at the door. I will discuss seven strategies. First, becoming ferociously other-centered in your interactions with a potential client. Second, avoiding looking ruthless to your potential client; you can show how you are ruthless in terms of getting the job done, but not in your dealings with the client. Third, having a growth mindset that allows you to treat the client and situation with compassion. Fourth, demonstrating to the potential client that both in mind and attitude you are the sole matter of importance to them right now. Fifth, demonstrating extreme patience and compassion when the potential client seems to be struggling during the conversation. Sixth, having an educator's mindset in which you implement a strategy where your number one priority in trust-building is showing the client (or other side in a negotiation) that your goal is to get a good understanding of the matter and then figure out the client or other side's role in solving the matter. Seventh, it is OK and, in fact, preferred that you are idiosyncratic, but do so in a manner that takes your unique skill set and personality and blends it with building a collaborative bond with the potential client.

1. **The concept of other-centeredness is crucial to building Insta-Trust.** Think of a time where you were the patient/client and a professional acted in a manner you perceived as arrogant. What were their arrogant cues? Facial expressions? Voice tone? Failure to listen or interruptions? Coming off as authoritative without being collaborative? Make a list of those arrogant traits that ticked you off. Ask yourself whether you have done the same thing in the past with your potential and actual clients. While everyone has bad days where our moods are far from perfect, that's no excuse. Does your trust-building performance fall short on the arrogance meter with any level of frequency? Take your prior bad experiences on the other side of the table as a client to examine and eliminate the manner in which you antagonize potential clients with your attitude. Become ferociously other-centered in your interactions with a potential client.

2. **The concept of ruthlessness is often not discussed in the context of client interactions.** On the one hand, your clients want you to be professionally ruthless in how you find solutions to their problems and represent their best interests. On the other hand, they are turned off by your demonstrating ruthlessness as a personality trait in front of them. So how do you demonstrate ruthlessness in an initial interaction with a client? You foreshadow it in your conversation. You have a collaborative conversation with the potential client, and at the point where you want to demonstrate

how aggressive you are going to be in representing them, you tell them you are about to show them how you are going be ferocious on their behalf. It could be through an example of your negotiation or litigation style. If it is a medical or dental matter, it could be through showing with confidence with gestures and movement (and with their X-rays or MRI if available) how you will get their job done. If you are an architect or engineer, you can use visual aids to show your creative side and tell them with enthusiasm how you want to help them with their project. Even CPAs have the ability to demonstrate enthusiasm and aggression in their interactions with potential clients by showing how they can help them save money or defend them against the IRS. The key to successfully using these aggressive approaches in an initial pitch is telling the client first what you are going to do and then after you do it, going back to collaborative mode and making it clear you are arrogant/aggressive on the problem, but not your relationship with them.

3. **Much professional arrogance arises because the professional truly believes that they are an expert in a specific subject matter and their expertise should be acknowledged and not challenged.** Truly gifted professionals have a growth mindset. They recognize there is always something more to learn about their subject matter. They go to conferences and learn about cutting-edge techniques and new strategies that can be used to help their clients. They also realize client interactions are potential growth experiences. When a professional has a growth mindset, it filters into their interactions with potential clients. When you have a growth mindset, you take the approach that you are on a learning journey with the potential client. When you think of potential client interactions as a learning journey, the trust gates open up wide because the client senses you might have the superior technical knowledge in the area of concern. And, your aura demonstrates a strong desire to learn about each other's interests in a process where the professional's expertise and the client's openness to expressing their concerns and issue result in a win-win solution for the client.

4. **Arrogance with clients often manifests itself through professional lack of concentration.** The professional gives the impression of listening to the client, but it becomes evident that their mind is wandering to other concerns. Visible lack of focus in front of the client (whether in a virtual or in-person setting) is probably the worst type of arrogance you can demonstrate. Lack of focus suggests to the client that they are not the most important

matter to you at the present and they will not be the important matter to you once you are hired. You can't blame the potential client for making that leap. If you feel you might not be adequately prepared for an initial meeting with a client, reschedule it. If you find yourself wandering during the middle of a meeting, call yourself out, profusely apologize and demonstrate during the rest of the meeting that you are super present. (And make sure you are not looking at your phone or another screen). If you consistently come to potential client meetings unfocused and ill prepared, your public reputation will be negatively impacted to a serious extent. So to show your ego is not an impediment to client service, focus, focus, focus on the potential client every single minute you are with them.

5. **When you think of arrogance or ego in a professional, how much do you focus on lack of patience?** The egotistical professional gives the impression that their time is very valuable and not to be wasted. In fact, failure to address time issues in a professional conversation is a huge obstacle to building Insta-Trust in an additional meeting. Time issues manifest themselves in several ways. First, part of an initial conversation involves understanding a client's expectations regarding the length of time a matter might take from start to finish. Building Insta-Trust requires the professional and client to have candid conversations about the time requirements associated with the matter and whether they are realistic. Second, failing to schedule an adequate amount of time for an initial client meeting can lead to your impatience, which gets quickly conveyed to the potential client. Good luck getting a client who thinks you are a clock watcher to retain you. Third, some potential clients are themselves impatient and you need to overcome their impatience when appropriate to make sure they understand the gravity of the matter and how hard you are trying to find out solutions that benefit them (rebutting their time impatience in a collaborative manner is a great way of showing them you care and building trust).

6. **At the beginning of this book, I stated that if you take an educator mindset into your trust-building encounters, you will have a high success rate in terms of client retention and satisfaction.** The Insta-Trust professional views the primary objectives in an initial client meeting as ultimately educating the potential client on the matter at hand, the gravity of the matter, the impact of the matter on them and one or more potential solutions that will help them. The professional who has an educator mindset is ferociously focused on educating themselves and their potential client

on matters of importance to both of them and the matter at hand. Think of one of your best professors. Your best professors wanted you to learn the subject matter, and they spent a lot of time putting together a syllabus and course schedule designed to maximize your learning. Their teaching method frequently blended technical knowledge with abstract learning designed to make you think like a doctor, dental specialist, attorney, CPA, architect, engineer, etc. Abstract learning processes require a strong understanding of facts and how to apply the technical skills you learned to a diverse range of settings. The same is true in professional settings. When you have a teaching mindset, you are fixated on helping the potential client learn about the matter at hand through your gentle guidance. They learn through your educating them, directly on the technical skills and more deftly through the use of active questioning to gather important facts. Importantly, like a great professor, you build a strong bond with a potential client by gently giving them the impression that you are an active partner in their success. Thinking like an educator allows you to treat the client and their problem as a matter where the student wants to be educated (but not lectured!) in a specific subject. The Insta-Trust approach is similar to a stellar educational process in that both involve substantial collaborative and frank interactions to educate each other about matters that lead to a win-win solution for both. The Insta-Trust professional focuses on using an educational process as a critical component of building client trust.

7. **Finally, most clients find it more interesting to work with a professional who exhibits a combination of personality, flair and technical expertise.** Personality does not have to equate with ego or arrogance. The professional who blends humor, stories and enthusiasm is more likely to gain the trust of a prospective client than one who comes across as overly technical and as primarily monotone. An idiosyncratic personality can come off as empathetic, collaborative and client-centered as long as the professional approach is not ego-driven. Client-centered enthusiasm gives potential clients the sense that you are more than a technical expert; you are a human with whom they can feel comfortable working. You obviously should not fake an idiosyncratic personality; if your personality is more taciturn, don't attempt to be someone who you aren't. But even if your personality is more reserved, in order to build Insta-Trust, please try to use targeted stories and enthusiasm to show the potential client your deep interest in them and their problem. You won't come off as egotistic but rather as client-centered.

"THE INSTA-TRUST PROFESSIONAL FOCUSES ON USING AN EDUCATIONAL PROCESS AS A CRITICAL COMPONENT OF BUILDING CLIENT TRUST."

– Dr. Larry Jacobson

Ego is your greatest barrier to building Insta-Trust. You know you are smart, but the way to demonstrate it is to turn your knowledge into a conversational approach that gently allows you to build trust and develop client-oriented solutions. Ask yourself and those who work with you to honestly assess those ego traits that you demonstrate when meeting a prospect. Have a clear and unmistakable mindset that you will use your intelligence to the serve and you are on the way to developing a strong Insta-Trust mindset.

This chapter will not contain an analysis of ego with respect to the various client archetypes. Demonstrable ego is counterproductive to developing strong client relationships regardless of personality type. There is not a prospective client out there who can benefit from a display of unbridled ego or even the subtle nonverbal signals that an egotist can send.

WHEELS OF INSTA-TRUST™:
Insta-Trust Impactor

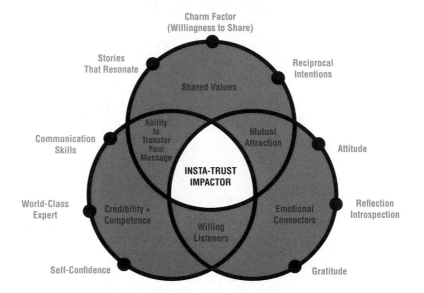

This chapter discusses the destructive role ego gone wild can do to destroy a professional's ability to develop Insta-Trust, in particular, when you demonstrate external ego. Look in the mirror hard and ask how arrogant you come off to others. The importance of the lack of external egocentricity is that you cannot become an Insta-Trust Impactor if external ego is your default personality in dealing with others. The Insta-Trust Impactor must master the ability to dig deep to find Shared Values with others. He or she must develop a Hall of Fame skill set in ascertaining the Emotional Connectors that resonate with the single individual sitting in front of you and do so by showing a can-do attitude and a sense of gratitude. Then, of course, you must demonstrate you can get the job done through exceptional Competence and have the Credibility to deliver what you promise. The Insta-Trust Impactor destroys their external ego and blends their use of Shared Values, Emotional Connectors skills and their Credibility and Competence as an integrated approach in dealing with other persons in new situations. The Insta-Trust Impactor relishes novelty, both in terms of dealing with people and technical problems. The dedicated Insta-Trust Impactor builds trust through understanding people as individuals and their real problems as deserving of the highest level of attention possible.

The following graph nicely summarizes the need to develop competency and interpersonal skills in becoming an Insta-Trust Impactor.

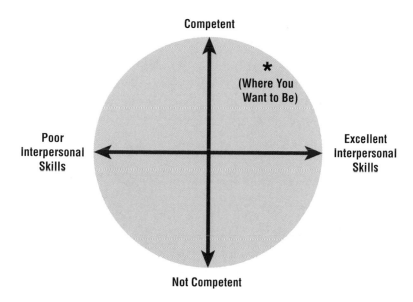

Starting in the top left quadrant, you are competent but lack the interpersonal skills I have described in this book. If you are competent, even highly competent, you might sometimes overlook your lack of empathy, communication skills and ability to connect on a human level, but the hard reality is that you will lack the client base and professional reputation that you could obtain if you applied the concepts in this book.

Moving down in the lower left quadrant, you are bereft of both competency and interpersonal skills. If you fit in this quadrant (and hopefully you don't), your ability to generate work is almost nonexistent. First, take the time to develop your interpersonal skills; you might be able to generate some work if people can relate to you even if your competency level is mediocre. But then to build Insta-Trust, you really need to build your competence to a higher level. You can't fool people for very long.

Moving to the lower right quadrant, you have excellent interpersonal skills but lack competency. Here your personal and professional solution is simple. Continue to enhance your interpersonal skills and become the most highly competent professional you can become.

Become a continuous and lifelong learner and view your potential clients and patients as you would your own family and close friends. Be the type of professional whom others would be proud to work with and refer to their own family and close friends.

Finally, we reach the top right quadrant where you have both excellent interpersonal skills and high competency. The place on the graph you want to be is the far northeast part of the top right quadrant where the star is located. Having exceptional interpersonal skills (including listening, gratitude, attitude, ability to communicate shared values and the ability to connect on an emotional level), coupled with high competence, is the sweet spot of the Insta-Trust Impactor. You have accomplished the Yin and Yang of becoming an exceptional professional. You have eliminated ego as a blocker for developing relationships. YOU HAVE BECOME THE INSTA-TRUST IMPACTOR.

Where do you fall on this graph? This graph is not a test; rather, it's a reality check. Be truthful with yourself. You know where you are and you can now see where you need to go.

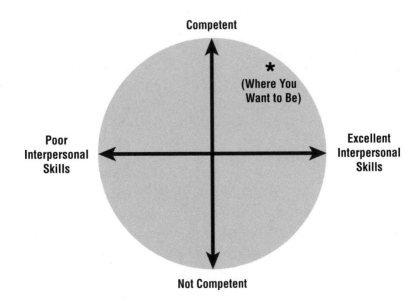

Ask Yourself

QUESTION ONE. Do I periodically do an ego check and make the appropriate adjustments if I am demonstrating verbal and nonverbal ego to prospective clients?

QUESTION TWO. Do I take active steps to NOT come off as the smartest person in the room?

QUESTION THREE. Do I display professional arrogance by using overly technical language with the prospective client?

QUESTION FOUR. Do I display professional arrogance by giving the impression that my time is more valuable than their time?

QUESTION FIVE. Do I unmistakably convey to the client that they are my sole focus during the entirety of our meeting?

QUESTION SIX. Do I have a growth educator mindset that allows me to take the prospective client on a trusting, collaborative and partnership-oriented problem-solving journey?

QUESTION SEVEN. Can I separate my idiosyncrasies from my ego and use them to Patricia's benefit to build trust in a highly interesting, yet professional, manner?

If you are ready to take your Insta-Trust skills to the next level, please go to www.insta-trust.com to obtain a free workbook that allows you to implement the important concepts discussed in this book.

THIS IS THE END, MY FRIEND

"And in the end, the trust you take is equal to the trust you make."
– Paraphrasing The Beatles

If you are ready to take your Insta-Trust skills to the next level, please go to www.insta-trust.com to obtain a free workbook that allows you to implement the important concepts discussed in this book.

Trust building in an initial professional interaction is really hard. There is no cookie-cutter formula in terms of how you build trust with a potential client or patient. You must have a deep toolbox that enables you to go with the flow depending on the personality type of the potential client and the direction in which the conversation moves. The questions at the end of Chapters Two through Ten are designed to make you think deeply about various aspects of conversations with potential clients that require you to develop bespoke trust-building approaches given the unique aspects of the interaction.

You have to unlearn bad habits first before you can learn Insta-Trust. Everyone has bad habits to discard, and many of them are trust breakers. Those bad habits can be so ingrained in our processes and personalities that it takes a substantial amount of self-reflection and practice over a period of time. Take your time to unlearn those bad habits that apply to you; they could be poor listening, lack of other-centeredness, subtle superiority traits or others. Once you have finished your unlearning process, then take positive steps to apply the concepts discussed in this book.

Make no mistake about it; without the development of some significant level of trust, the likelihood that you will be retained by the patient or client is slim. Sure there are rare circumstances of great importance where a desperate or highly knowledgeable individual might hire an arrogant, condescending or egotistical professional simply because their abilities are so superior and evident that the client is willing to put up with the professional because of the consequences involved. But neither you nor I are not the type of professional that can get away with such arrogance and develop a high-quality client base. In order to serve your communities with a high degree of competence and integrity, you must make it the highest priority to develop Insta-Trust skills of the highest magnitude. Your job, during the initial stages of an initial interaction, is, to quote the late Jim Morrison, to LIGHT THEIR FIRE. For if you can light their fire, you can move on to the technical aspects of the discussion and really begin the process of helping them with their problem.

"YOU HAVE TO UNLEARN BAD HABITS FIRST BEFORE YOU CAN LEARN INSTA-TRUST."

– Dr. Larry Jacobson

Think of when you ate at a diner restaurant for the first time. The likelihood is that your expectation of service was incredibly low compared to the first-class restaurants you have eaten. Yet, the waiter at the diner was very personable and gave you incredible service during your meal. In other words, he or she vastly exceeded expectations regarding the service provided and attitude conveyed. Aside from the likelihood that you gave the server a really big tip (you better have left a big tip), the fact that the service far exceeded expectations makes you want to have that server again if you ever go back to that diner.

Have that same mindset where you try to exceed the expectations of your prospective clients. Meeting their expectations is not enough if you want to earn their trust. Being nice, polite and earnest is not enough. Within the first three to five minutes of a new client interaction, the client has to feel that you are a person that they are willing to open up to and have them perform an important task or procedure for you. You have to light their fire.

In tying together the concepts discussed in this book, there are three overarching and broad concepts that are required to build Insta-Trust. They are Attitude, Reflection and Gratitude, easily remembered as ARG. If you master ARG, you will build world-class Insta-Trust with your potential clients. It is as simple as that.

ATTITUDE-TRAVEL THE YELLOW BRICK ROAD

You are already technically strong in the area that is of interest to the potential client. Yet if you were to give a client truth serum and ask them what made them hire you in the first place, the odds are very high that they would have said you have a can-do attitude. What are the components of a can-do attitude? Friendliness, of course. A personality that tells the other person that you are deeply committed to helping them solve their problem. An approach that is warm, not arrogant or off-putting. All of these characteristics are important to building Insta-Trust, and you should strive to demonstrate friendliness, commit to them and avoid arrogance. But there is one aspect of attitude that is important above all others.

You absolutely need to convey to the potential client that you are their partner during the journey to solve their problem and alleviate their pain. Yes, they want to see you are committed to them, but they need you to show, by word and deed, that you are on a journey together. You will travel the yellow brick road, like Dorothy, the Scarecrow, the Tin Man and the Cowardly Lion. When they traveled into the unknown, they spent time learning about each other, and when the road became tough, they supported each other. Like the characters in *The Wizard of Oz*, you want your prospective clients to think that you are partners on a journey that will lead to finding what they are looking for at the end of the process.

In conveying a partnership-type attitude, you need to take prospective clients as you find them in terms of their personality. Study their personality archetype and modify your approach depending on their attitude. You need to adjust to their personality. They are likely not going to care about where you went to school or where you did your postgraduate training. They are not going to care about your personal or professional problems.

All they care about is whether you demonstrate, clearly and with enthusiasm, that you deeply care about them as a person and that your care will carry over in terms of the enthusiasm you will show when you are working on their matter.

Follow the Yellow Brick Road with your new client.

REFLECTION-YOU WON'T GET FOOLED AGAIN

As discussed earlier, we frequently are quite dense as to how we interact with others. Through confirmation bias and sheer inattentiveness, you and I are ignorant as to how condescending and superior we can appear to others. Your staff and associates frequently do not have the guts to tell you when you come off as smug to a potential patient. It is your personal responsibility to improve your trust-building skills. You do that through continuous self-reflection. Self-reflection is not meditation and it doesn't need to involve therapy.

Self-reflection involves deliberate practice as to how to improve your trust-building skills. There are several approaches that you can take. First, with a prospective patient or client you can have an associate take notes and then at the end of the day you can briefly discuss with them how things went well and how they can be improved from an interpersonal standpoint. Second, you can hire a coach to spend time with you during client (potential, new and veteran) interactions and receive highly professional feedback regarding your trust-building skills. Third, and lastly, you can keep a journal where daily you spend a few minutes reflecting back on what you did that was positive and negative in terms of client interactions. The journaling doesn't have to be lengthy, but it should be done on a consistent basis as otherwise the reflective nature of the exercise tends to get lost.

The trusted professional is a reflective professional. You step into the growth mindset of continuous improvement when it comes to enhancing trust-building interpersonal skills with new and existing clients. Reflection allows you to remain client-centered in your approach. Reflection makes you see how you want to present yourself to clients. And reflection enables you be the best combination of your interpersonal and technical selves to serve your clients to their maximum benefit.

Dr. Larry Jacobson

GRATITUDE-THE REAL ME

Why do you get up in the morning? Of course, you have a family that you love and want to serve in a warm way. You have to earn money in order to serve your family's material, psychological and spiritual needs. Turning to your professional sphere, you take great pride in the quality of your work for clients. I always viewed myself as a professional innovator who has used the law and my negotiating skills to create elegant and positive solutions for my clients.

Yet our professional rewards should be more than material or psychic. Don't get me wrong, material and psychic rewards help during the dog days that we all face periodically during our careers. Not every day in our careers is wine and roses; another way, beyond high-level trust skills, that a high-quality professional remains a high-quality professional is the manner in which he or she copes with the inevitable lows of their practice. But that is a topic for another book. The highly skilled professional has a career aspiration of serving with gratitude.

The real me, meaning the professional that you would want to represent you, has a strong sense of gratitude. Gratitude for the time spent honing technical skills. Gratitude for the people you work with and the manner in which you can help them become better at their jobs and other aspects of their lives. But the most important element of professional gratitude involves the immense satisfaction you get from serving your clients or patients—from using your ability to save a person's life, alleviate their pain (and the pain you are helping to cure can be physical, psychological, material or spiritual) or solve an important problem for them. You can serve your client by selling their business in a painless and profitable manner. You can help clients build beautiful structures that house businesses, factories, airports, schools or other organizations. You can solve their business problems or get the IRS off their back. You can invent something that can improve the lives of thousands or millions of people.

Professionals who embody gratitude toward clients generate the highest amount of trust from clients and potential clients. Clients can see it and they can feel it. There are two types of gratitude: internal gratitude, where you feel down in your bones that your purpose in life is to serve your clients, and external gratitude, where you externally show your clients how much it means to you to serve them to the absolute best of your ability. Maximum Insta-Trust is generated when you have internal gratitude and show external gratitude. You see, when you have internal gratitude toward serving your potential clients, that begins to manifest itself in external gratitude. You still have to use the tools discussed in this book to verbally and nonverbally demonstrate external gratitude, but if you start from a point of high internal gratitude, it is far easier to display external gratitude toward those you serve. Gratitude, internal and external, allows your potential clients to see you in the most favorable light possible.

You and I have come full circle. I thank you for joining me on this journey. I am grateful for your honoring me by getting to the end of this book. Serving clients with strong interpersonal panache and high technical skill is the highest honor any of us can achieve. But to serve clients, you have to get them first. View initial client interactions as a fun and important step to serving them. You begin to serve them by building Insta-Trust early in the first conversation you have with them. Assess their personality, diagnose their problem and develop solutions for them. Do it in a collaborative manner that respects them in terms of their mindset and skill level. To paraphrase The Beatles, in the end the trust you ultimately take is equal to the trust you make. If you build a reservoir of Insta-Trust at the beginning of the relationship, the accumulation of trust will allow you to take some of that built-up trust to smooth over the inevitable rough patches you will face. Build a huge reservoir of Insta-Trust and serve your new clients with gratitude, pride and excellence. Your clients—and the world—will be better off because of your newfound Insta-Trust skill set.

CODA

"If you build it, they will come."
— Field of Dreams

My wife and I had the honor of attending the first Field of Dreams Major League Baseball game between the White Sox and the Yankees. The whole experience was filled with nostalgia, scenic beauty and great baseball. But the highlight of the evening was Kevin Costner, who played a farmer who built a baseball field in the movie *Field of Dreams*. Costner entered the playing field, walking in from the cornfields in the outfield. He walked in slowly and must have taken five minutes to reach the infield. It was clear that the emotional aspect of the moment made him genuinely move in a deliberate manner. After he stopped walking, he calmly and authoritatively told the crowd about the movie and its impact not only on him, but on millions of devoted movie watchers. His aura was so powerful that the players on the White Sox and the Yankees were mesmerized by his words and presence. Costner could have asked the crowd to do anything and we would have complied.

Why? Simply because Costner built trust with the crowd and the players within the first 60 seconds of walking onto the field. Yes, he is a movie superstar, but that wasn't it. It was because he exuded quiet confidence by walking and talking slowly. He spoke to the crowd in an authoritative tone, but not in a demeaning way. He blended the right type of nostalgia with a narrative of how baseball is still important. In other words, he quickly built Insta-Trust through a combination of his superb narrative skills and making the crowd feel what he felt—that baseball and its fans have a key role in history and the present. And the White Sox players gave him high fives after he was finished with his entry.

Use Kevin Costner as your guidepost. When you are in a new situation, build trust by speaking to your audience with quiet confidence and competence. For if you can use your quiet confidence to create a collaborative discussion with new patients or clients, they will come to you with enthusiasm and hope.

ACKNOWLEDGMENTS

The genesis of this book arguably goes back over 40 years to when I started practicing law as a young attorney. Since 1981, whether as an attorney or as a practice transition consultant to oral surgeons, I have always been fascinated with how professionals gain the trust of their patients or clients. The 1980s and 1990s were a far different period: there was no social media, the Internet was in its infancy, there was little or no video conferencing, and people actually liked to meet face-to-face. The technological changes of the last 20 years or so have led to a skepticism among individuals that has made it far more difficult to break through and build trust with anyone, but especially in the professional realm. So the first people I would like to thank are the thousands of clients whom I have had the pleasure of representing and the thousands of attorneys and deal makers with whom I have had the pleasure of negotiating over the years. I have learned a lot from you and am honored to have worked with you.

A singular individual was responsible for my not only becoming a first-class tax attorney, but also developing as a mensch. The late Martin Ginsburg started teaching tax law at Georgetown in the fall of 1980, when he moved to Washington, D.C., with his wife, Ruth Bader Ginsburg, who had been appointed to the D.C. Circuit as a federal appeals judge. I took his first class, a corporate tax seminar that started with 16 students and ended with 4. Marty basically shaped my life. To this day, he is the most brilliant person I have ever encountered. More importantly, he was also arguably the kindest and most generous attorney I have ever met (and the professional sacrifices he was so eager and enthusiastic to make to support his wife are well known). Beyond tax law, Marty taught us to see the "big picture," which included not only the technical aspects of the law but also the interpersonal aspects of a given situation (which in the case of our class involved trying to convince jaded Congressional staff members of much-needed tax law changes). I would not be where I am today without having Marty as a professor and guide.

When I decided that I needed a change in professional direction, I undertook two steps. The first was to attend a master's program in Organizational Dynamics at the University of Pennsylvania. At Penn, we took courses that were designed to help us understand organizations, organizational behavior and individual behavior through the lens of the liberal arts. It was at Penn that I learned systems theory, and a good part of the material in this book is based upon my personal interpretation of systems theory as treating an individual as his or her own complex system that needs to be evaluated in terms of developing relationships. So at this point, I would like to thank my professors at the University of Pennsylvania, with a particular shout-out to Peter Steiner, my thesis advisor and one of the most well-rounded and interesting people with whom I have ever had the pleasure of working.

The second step in my change of professional direction was attending Creighton University and obtaining my doctorate. I was honored to be influenced by many professors, but a few deserve personal recognition. Dr. Donna Ehrlich was my doctoral advisor and provided me with great insight regarding the importance of research. Dr. Isabelle Cherney was the head of my program at the time of my attendance, and she was kind enough to encourage me to come to Creighton, even though my research interests did not completely align with the program's focus. Most of all, I would like to thank Jacqueline N. Font-Guzmán. Jackie was my thesis advisor and encouraged me to delve deeply, from a research perspective, into trust building with new counterparties. My thesis—and to a great extent, the content of this book—is due to her guidance on what is and isn't important when it comes to thinking about fast trust in professional settings. Thanks, Jackie!

When I decided I was finally ready to write my first book in 2021, during the middle of a pandemic no less, I attended a workshop presented by Jeffrey and Jennifer Gitomer. They blew me away with their passion, their intelligence and their knowledge of what makes a great book. After the workshop, I decided to work with

Jeffrey and Jen one on one to get this book written and published. I thought writing a doctoral dissertation was tough; Jeffrey and Jen used tough love to get me to see that academic and legal writing are far different than writing for a general audience. They guided me through draft after draft. Jeffrey's insight into human behavior is off the charts. Jen's insight as to what makes a great read is of Hall of Fame caliber. They make a great team, and I can truly say this book would not have happened without their commitment to me and the process. The best thing I can say about writing this book is the personal relationship I developed with Jeffrey and Jen, and I deeply thank them for all they did for me.

I would also like to thank Michael Wolff for his brilliant book design and David Wildasin for taking on a first-time author as my publisher. I am deeply appreciative of all that both of you have done for me in this process.

From a personal standpoint, I could literally thank hundreds of friends and family members, but I am not going to turn this into an Oscars acceptance speech. For those I have not thanked publicly for helping me develop personally and professionally, you know who you are and thank you.

A special thanks goes to Michael Lufrano. We served together as board members at the school I referenced in the book. We worked together intimately on several major projects that completely changed the direction of the school. I learned so much from Mike; he was the person who taught me that "you take the other person as you find them" and adapt to them rather than forcing your personality on them. He also happens to be one of the nicest people you will ever meet. Had it not been for him (and Marty Ginsburg and Jackie Font), my personal development would have taken a different path and this book would not have been written. Thanks, Mike!

The next thank you goes to Erica Wexler. Erica and I met at Penn in 2008 on a class trip to Paris. Like me, Erica has a bespoke outlook on life; we look at each new situation as an original challenge and treat clients (whether new or existing) as people and organizations that deserve a fresh perspective in terms of problem solving. Her insights into this book were entirely reader-centric and helped shape many of the major themes discussed. Erica is a cherished friend and business colleague, and I look forward to working with her for many years in the future on our joint business endeavors.

Last, but most important, comes family. My daughter Sara and son Daniel have to put up with a father who can be challenging and idiosyncratic. Sara and Dan have made me better people. I have tried (not always with success) to be more patient around them. They have taught me that being other-centered is even more important in family relationships than professional relationships. They have their own professional lives, and I am deeply proud of their professional and personal achievements. My love for them is boundless.

As for my wife Cindy, she has always been my number one cheerleader and supporter. She has been with me for the good, the bad and the ugly, and she has always been a rock of stability. As family and friends know, Cindy is probably the most giving person they will ever encounter. She has certainly given me a hell of a lot more than I have given her. My life would be incomplete without Cindy. Due to Cindy's belief in me, I have been able to achieve a level of personal and professional contentment that would have been impossible otherwise. My love for her is unconditional.

Dr Lj

Dr. Larry Jacobson